CHRISTIANITY or HUMANISM

Which Will You Choose?

ROBERT L. WAGGONER, D.MIN.

Robert L. Waggoner

Publishing Designs, Inc.

Publishing Designs, Inc.
P.O. Box 3241
Huntsville, Alabama 35810

© 2007 Robert L. Waggoner, D.Min.

All rights reserved. No part of this book may be reproduced or transmitted without written permission from Publishing Designs except for the inclusion of short quotations in a review.

All scripture quotations, unless otherwise indicated, are taken from the New King James Version. Copyright © 1982 by Thomas Nelson, Inc. Used by permission. All rights reserved.

Library of Congress Cataloging-in-Publication Data

Waggoner, Robert L., 1931-
  Christianity or humanism : BLURB : which will you choose? / Robert L. Waggoner.
     p. cm.
  Includes index.
  ISBN 978-0-929540-67-2 (alk. paper)
  1. Apologetics. 2. Christianity. 3. Humanism. I. Title.
BT1103.W34 2007
261.2'1-dc22
                            2007044229

Printed in the United States

To my son, Clark (whom I love dearly), who as a teen-ager, indirectly motivated me to search for answers to many questions, most of which I could not then even begin to formulate.

CONTENTS

Acknowledgments 7
Preface 9
Introduction 13
  1. Religion 17
  2. Philosophy. 35
  3. History. 47
  4. Ethics. 57
  5. Biology. 67
  6. Medicine 77
  7. Psychology 87
  8. Sociology. 97
  9. Law 107
10. Politics 117
11. Economics. 129
12. Education 139
13. Culture. 151
Summary. 161
What Christians Can Do 164
Suggested Readings. 166
Indices
    Name Index 168
    Scripture Index 169
    Subject Index 170

ACKNOWLEDGMENTS

Over twenty-five years ago, I discovered the philosophy of secular Humanism—after I had been preaching for over twenty-five years! To my horror, I discovered that secular Humanism is the primary philosophical enemy of Christianity, that it dominates almost all aspects of life not only in our nation but also throughout the world, and that I had been totally unaware of it. I wondered why I had not known about this before. Why had Christian leaders not been alert to teach against this anti-Christian philosophical enemy? When I began to talk about secular Humanism, only a very few of my church friends had any idea what I was talking about.

Lottie Beth Hobbs

I discovered secular Humanism when I began to receive an unsolicited periodical called *Pro-Family Forum* from Lottie Beth Hobbs. It was an eight-page publication about what's happening in our world. (Lottie Beth realized that preachers and other church leaders needed to know the dangers of Humanism; she determined to inform them.) Every issue of her publication included order forms for books on topics discussed. I began to order some books. As I read them, I began to express ideas contained in them. Most people did not believe me, partly because I did not express those ideas very well, and partly because they were hearing something very different from their understandings of reality. I began to document my discoveries. Slowly these ideas began to gain credibility among my church friends. Thank you, Lottie Beth Hobbs, for your influence upon my thinking.

Dr. David Noebel

One of the most comprehensive books that later came to my attention was David Noebel's book, *Understanding the Times: The Story of the Biblical Christian, Marxist/Leninist, and Secular Humanist Worldviews*. Following two introductory chapters, this book treats ten categories, each considers three perspectives—biblical Christianity, Marxist/Leninism, and secular Humanism—with one chapter to each perspective. A lengthy closing chapter then relates each of the ten categories to the New Age philosophy. I found Noebel's book extremely helpful. I mention it here because it provided significant background that ultimately influenced the writing of this book. Thank you, Dr. David Noebel.

Dr. Pat Hardeman, Dr. Phillip Slate, and Dr. Bert Thompson

I began writing notes for *Christianity or Humanism* about a decade ago. More than three years ago, I placed a draft in the hands of some friends and colleagues for their evaluations and critiques. Dr. Pat Hardeman, Dr. Phillip Slate, and Dr. Bert Thompson had very beneficial suggestions, many of which I've incorporated into this book. Thank you, Dr. Hardeman, Dr. Slate, and Dr. Thompson. Criticisms of this work that may be forthcoming should be directed only to me—not to any of these scholars.

Friends, Associates, Scholars

I'm thankful for the many, many friends and associates who have encouraged and supported me in my study, writing, and teaching about the devastating influences of secular Humanism in our culture and upon the church. I'm also very grateful to a host of scholars from many fields whose written works have furnished me with excellent insight regarding conflicts between biblical Christianity and secular Humanism. As the writings of others have blessed my life and provided me a better understanding of the spiritual battle between biblical Christianity and secular Humanism that rages in our world, so also my hope is that this book will be a blessing to the lives of many others.

Publishing Designs, Inc.

Research and writing are an author's responsibility, but additional expertise is needed to market a book. I'm grateful to James Andrews, Peggy Coulter, and the staff at Publishing Designs for their expertise in giving grand style and aesthetic attractiveness of my manuscript to the public.

PREFACE

Since many professed Christians know little, if anything, about secular Humanism, they may think it is not necessary to prove that biblical Christianity is superior. Such thinking reveals this: They have been greatly humanized without their being aware of it! Many professed Christians in our modern world are unaware that our whole culture now operates more by the values of secular Humanism than it does by the principles of biblical Christianity. Even if a majority of our culture professes to be Christian, the quality of Christianity for most is so weak that it is essentially not identifiable with biblical Christianity. Therefore, their weak Christianity has little power to resist the assaults of secular Humanism.

The perspectives of biblical Christianity and secular Humanism must be contrasted to show that (1) the two cannot coexist in a stable society, (2) their respective values are constantly at war with each other in a presumed secular society, and (3) biblical Christianity is superior to secular Humanism in every way.

While Christians generally realize there are differences between Christian and Humanist perspectives—theological, philosophical, and ethical—many seem unaware that there are also distinctive Christian perspectives regarding such subjects as history, law, politics, education, and economics. That Christians are not generally aware of distinctive Christian perspectives in these latter categories is but an indication that secular Humanism has captured Christian thinking to the point that many Christians no longer realize they should have a distinctive Christian mindset regarding every subject.

Criteria acceptable to both Christians and Humanists are required to demonstrate superiority. While Christians are willing to prove that Christianity is consistent with divine revelation, secular Humanists discount all biblical evidence. Therefore since secular Humanists accept those things which are scientific, reasonable, and according to critical intelligence, our objective is to demonstrate that biblical Christianity is superior to secular Humanism according to their criteria. Biblical Christianity is consistent with divine revelation.

The relevance of this study may be emphasized by quoting from Harry Blamires, who made the following observation in 1963:

> There is no longer a Christian mind. It is commonplace that the mind of modern man has been secularized. For instance, it has been deprived of any orientation towards the supernatural. Tragic as this fact is, it would not be so desperately tragic had the Christian mind held out against the secular drift. But unfortunately the Christian mind has succumbed to the secular drift with a degree of weakness and nervelessness unmatched in Christian history. It is difficult to do justice in words to the complete loss of intellectual morale in the twentieth-century Church. One cannot characterize it without having recourse to language which will sound hysterical and melodramatic.
>
> There is no longer a Christian mind. There is still, of course, a Christian ethic, a Christian practice, and a Christian spirituality. As a moral being, the modern Christian subscribes to a code other than that of the non-Christian. As a member of the Church, he undertakes obligations and observations ignored by the non-Christian. As a spiritual being, in prayer and meditation, he strives to cultivate a dimension of life unexplored by the non-Christian. But as a *thinking* being, the modern Christian has succumbed to secularization. He accepts religion—its morality, its worship, its spiritual culture—but he rejects the religious view of life, the view which sets all earthly issues within the context of the eternal view which relates all human problems—social, political, cultural—to the doctrinal foundations of the Christian Faith, the view which sees all things here below in terms of God's supremacy and earth's transitoriness, in terms of Heaven and Hell.[1]

Christians, because of eternal consequences, are concerned to demonstrate the superiority of Christian beliefs over Humanist beliefs. Those concerns are of no interest to Humanists, because they are concerned only about what is here and now. Therefore,

---

[1] *The Christian Mind: How Should a Christian Think?* (Ann Arbor, MI: Servant Books), 3–4.

PREFACE

the superiority of Christian faith over secular Humanism must be shown as a better way of living in the here and now—better in the sense that a society which possesses Christian beliefs is stronger, more stable, and longer lasting than is a society which possesses Humanist beliefs.

Although written primarily for Christians, this book will be read by many Humanists. The purpose of this work is not only to inform but also to stimulate thought on the relevance of God and Christian values in all aspects of human life. Churches that use this book in adult class programs will receive great benefits.

This study will generate much discussion, because many Christians have never thought about these issues from a distinctively Christian point of view. In the thinking process, many will change their minds—some, several times. Not everyone will agree with everything I've set forth, but all who profess to be Christians should grapple with these issues and their implications. Christians must learn to think, not from secular, but from Christian perspectives. Many Christians may challenge some of the categorical distinctions and concepts given here between biblical Christianity and secular Humanism. Some challenges will arise because issues may be unfamiliar and therefore not clearly understood. Other challenges may arise from those who have given much study to these distinctions yet sincerely disagree. The affirmations presented here were not reached without considerable personal mental struggle. Your conclusions may be different from mine, but that's all right if we can arrive at a more Christian way of thinking. When enough professed Christians realize the strengths of biblical Christianity and the weaknesses of secular Humanism, they will become more galvanized in their faith and begin to discard Humanist values from society.

Christians must learn how their philosophical enemies think. They should read basic documents of Humanism, such as *Humanist Manifesto I, II,* and *III*. Christians should also read from Christian thinkers. A select list of general reading materials is provided on page 166. Also, recommended reading lists are included after several topics. Questions following each topic will provide review and promote class discussion.

Robert L. Waggoner, D.Min.
Montgomery, Alabama
October 2007

INTRODUCTION

A contrast between biblical Christianity and secular Humanism necessarily requires an understanding of terms. The documents of the New Testament will be used as a basis for understanding biblical Christianity. Basic documents of Humanism will be used as a basis for understanding the secular worldview. Christians do not always agree with other Christians; neither do Humanists always agree with each other. Christians' beliefs and Humanists' beliefs are considered in a general sense in this book. What Christians believe is generally founded upon biblical documents. What Humanists believe is generally founded upon the published writings by Humanists.

Because Renaissance Humanism is not the same as secular or contemporary Humanism, a brief explanation is in order regarding how Humanism is designated in this book. Renaissance Humanism may be designated by not capitalizing the word; secular or contemporary Humanism may be recognized by the term being capitalized. This distinction is reasonable because contemporary Humanism should be recognized as religious. Inasmuch as religions are designated by their terms being capitalized—Christian, Buddhist, Hindu—the term designating the religion of Humanism should also be capitalized. Also, since *Christian* is capitalized when referring to a believer in Christianity, *Humanist* will be capitalized when referring to a believer in contemporary Humanism.

Definition and History

Humanism may be defined as "any system or mode of thought or action in which human interests, values, and dignity predominate." Humanism consists of "a variety of ethical theory and practice that emphasizes reason, scientific inquiry, and human fulfillment in the natural world, and often rejects the importance of belief in God."[1] The definition of Humanism has changed since the time of the Renaissance when it related to devotion to or study

---

1 Random House Webster's Unabridged Dictionary

of the humanities. Secular Humanism may be defined as a philosophical perspective that removes God from reality and makes man the judge of all things.

Until the middle of twentieth century, the Christian faith dominated societies in the Western world. Now Christianity is seriously challenged on every hand by the growing worldview of secular Humanism. Ancient Greek Humanism, already in decay, was suppressed by the coming of Christianity. Christian values then came to govern social values in the Western world for nearly two thousand years. Only with the coming of the Renaissance in the sixteenth century were Christian beliefs and values challenged, and then only mildly at first. Renaissance humanists generally believed in God, the inspiration of the Bible, miracles, the deity of Christ, resurrection of the dead, divine judgment, and eternal destiny. But as Renaissance humanists studied literary works of humanity that did not relate to biblical truths, they started accepting anti-biblical values.

The so-called "Age of Enlightenment"—a misnomer because it presumes human enlightenment by reasoning apart from a knowledge of God—from the early 1600s until the late 1700s further expanded departures from biblical moorings. However, the greatest negative impact upon Christian values escalated after 1859 with the ever-increasing popularity of the theory of evolution. The result is that secular Humanists now deny the existence and relevancy of God, inspiration of the Bible, miracles, deity of Christ, resurrection of the dead, divine judgment, eternal destiny, and many other spiritual matters.

Secular Humanism may be designated by philosophical terms like secularism, naturalism, materialism, scientism, statism, socialism, egalitarianism, feminism, relativism, hedonism, rationalism, romanticism, multiculturalism, and globalism.

Humanism functions in many areas: religion, philosophy, history, ethics, biology, medicine, psychology, sociology, law, politics, economics, education, and culture. Differences between Christian and secular Humanist beliefs and values are presented in chapters

INTRODUCTION

by these categories, and Christian superiority over secular Humanism is demonstrated.

Religion and Culture

The basic issue is this: Can religion be separated from human life? Humanists think so! Yet, throughout recorded history no culture has been known that had absolutely no form of religion or worship. There are two approaches to relating religion and culture. One is to incorporate religion into all aspects of the culture. The other is to deny as fully as possible the right of religious beliefs to influence culture.

During most of human history, religious beliefs and practices have dominated all aspects of human existence. Until the sixteenth century, everyone realized that religion influences every aspect of human life. The concept of the secular apart from religion did not exist in human history. Only since the Renaissance has there been a growing effort to remove religious influence from culture.

The Conflict

The present conflict in beliefs and values is real. People have to make choices in their beliefs and behavior. We must choose between:

- creation and evolution.
- pro-life and pro-choice.
- acceptance and denial of the inspiration of Scripture.
- acceptance and rejection of the supernatural.
- a monistic and a dualistic view of humanity.
- human and divine ethics.
- capitalism and socialism.
- internationalism and globalism.

The consequences of these clashes are already upon us, as seen in the changes of social, legal, and cultural norms. However, future generations will feel greater consequences than can be presently imagined. Either Christianity will suppress secular Humanism and bring about a better society, or secular Humanism will suppress Christianity and produce national chaos and Christian persecution. The outcome is by no means certain. If Christians do not actively engage in this conflict, Christianity may be annihilated in this country.

Anyone who attempts to resolve conflicts between Christians and Humanists must realize that no solution can result from considering only one category of the conflict. The categories discussed are interrelated—some to a greater extent than others. Any ideological and practical solution to conflicts in one area must relate to resolving conflicts in other areas also.

The final section of each chapter is "Playing with Fire," an illustrative story intended to reinforce the message of the chapter. No person or event described in "Playing with Fire" is actual. A geographical area, when named in the story, is designated for the purpose of accommodating the fictitious events and characters.

Why Biblical Christianity Is Superior to Secular Humanism

CATEGORY	Biblical Christianity	or	Secular Humanism
Religion	Historical	or	Natural
Philosophy	Supernaturalism	or	Naturalism
History	From Creation to End of World	or	Evolutionary
Ethics	Absolute	or	Relative
Biology	Created	or	Evolved
Medicine	Pro-Life	or	Pro-Choice
Psychology	Dualism	or	Monism
Sociology	Family	or	Government
Law	Natural & Biblical Law	or	Positive Law
Politics	Justice & Freedom	or	Globalism
Economics	Stewardship	or	Socialism
Education	Family	or	Government
Culture	Theism	or	Secularism
SUMMARY	God	or	Man

CHAPTER

RELIGION

It cannot be emphasized too strongly or too often that this great nation was founded, not by religionists, but by Christians; not on religions, but on the Gospel of Jesus Christ. For this very reason peoples of other faiths have been afforded asylum, prosperity, and freedom of worship here.[1]

—**Patrick Henry**

Is Humanism a Religion?

Many Humanists do not admit that Humanism is a religion, but evidence proves it is. After proving Humanism is a religion and contrasting it with Christianity, we will demonstrate that the Christian religion is superior to the religion of Humanism.

Humanism Claims to Be a Religion

As the saying goes, if a bird looks like a duck, quacks like a duck, waddles like a duck, and swims like a duck, then it must be a duck. Likewise, if contemporary Humanism claims to be a religion, is legally declared to be a religion, and acts like a religion, then it must be a religion. This is true even though Humanists who

---

1 William J. Federer, *America's God and Country: Encyclopedia of Quotations* (Coppell, TX: FAME Publishing, Inc., 1994), 289.

previously affirmed that Humanism is a religion now deny it.[1] Evidence is available to refute all claims by Humanists when they say Humanism is not a religion.

The language of *Humanist Manifesto I* proves that its signors believed Humanism is a religion. They thought the circumstances of their world had "created a situation which requires a new statement of the means and purposes of religion."[2] They believed that "to establish such a religion is a major necessity of the present."[3] They declared: "In order that religious Humanism may be better understood we, the undersigned, desire to make certain affirmations which we believe the facts of our contemporary life demonstrate."[4]

Humanist Manifesto I affirmed fifteen principles, eight of which use language that requires recognition that Humanism is a religion.[5] The last paragraph of that document begins with the words: "So stands the theses of religious Humanism."[6]

Forty years after *Humanist Manifesto I* was written, Paul Kurtz declared in the opening statement in the preface to *Humanist Manifesto I and II* that "Humanism is a philosophical, religious, and moral point of view as old as human civilization itself."[7] He also stated that "in 1933 a group of thirty-four liberal Humanists in the United States defined and enunciated the philosophical and religious principles that seemed to them fundamental. They drafted *Humanist Manifesto I* . . . It was concerned with expressing a general religious and philosophical outlook . . ."[8]

---

1 See, for example, Paul Kurtz, "The New Inquisition in the Schools," *Free Inquiry*. Winter, 1986/87, 5.
2 Paul Kurtz, ed. *Humanist Manifestoes I and II* (Buffalo, NY: Promotheus Books. 1973), 8.
3 Ibid.
4 Ibid., 7.
5 These are numbered First, Fifth, Seventh, Eighth, Ninth, Tenth, Twelfth, and Thirteenth.
6 Kurtz, 10.
7 Ibid., 3.
8 Ibid.

Kurtz then noted that *Humanist Manifesto II* also addressed itself to "the problems of religion."[9] The first two of seventeen statements of belief in *Humanist Manifesto II* are discussed under the category of Religion. Although the language of "religious Humanism" is not used in the second manifesto as extensively as it was in the first, there can be no doubt that the beliefs presented in the second document may also be categorized as "religious Humanism."[10]

Moreover, the *Bylaws of the American Humanist Association* declare that "the American Humanist Association was incorporated under the 'not for profit act' of the State of Illinois as a non-profit organization, as certified by the Articles of Incorporation dated 13 February 1943, which Articles were amended 20 March 1968, to reflect that the Association has a legal status as a 'religious organization.'"[11]

 The American Humanist Association has a legal status as a religious organization.

Humanism Has Been Legally Declared to Be a Religion

In the traditional Christian sense, religion is God-centered. Atheism, being opposed to a belief in God, is man-centered, and until recently was not considered as a religion. It is now.

> Beginning in the 1940s, Christian theism came under increasing attack. The federal courts began to broaden and diversify the definition of *religion* until by the end of the 1960s the judicial definition

---

9 Kurtz, 3.
10 For a good evaluation and comparison of basic Humanists' writings, see Norman L. Geisler. *Is Man the Measure: An Evaluation of Contemporary Humanism* (Grand Rapids: Baker Book House. 1983), especially chapter 9, "Secular Humanism," 111–122.
11 *Bylaws of the American Humanist Association*, enacted 1971; revised 1977; amended 1978, 1980. Update compilation, July, 1981 by the subcommittee on American Humanist Association Bylaws: Harvey Lebrum, Ward Tabler, Howard Consalves, "Historical Note," 1.

of religion was altered from *sustenance of belief* (belief in and obligation owed to the "Creator") to the *impact* of the belief on the *life* of the person expressing and holding it . . . The basis of truth was shifting from Christian theism's emphasis on God-centered-ness to Humanism's emphasis on man-centered-ness.[1]

The courts' alteration of the definition of religion resulted in religion's finally being defined as "ultimate concern."[2] That is, whatever is of ultimate concern to an individual is his religion. This in turn led to the court's definition of Humanism as religion. In the landmark case of *Torcaso v. Watkins,* the U.S. Supreme Court said that "among religions in this country which do not teach what would generally be considered a belief in the existence of God are Buddhism, Taoism, Ethical Culture, Secular Humanism and others."[3] Other court decisions have also declared that Humanism is a religion.[4]

Do contemporary Humanists deny that Humanism is a religion because they realize that if Humanism is generally considered to be a religion, then it, like Christianity, is also subject to the First Amendment's prohibition of the establishment of religion, and therefore may not be taught in public schools? Many Christians believe that Humanism is a religion and that it dominates the philosophical foundations and psychological methodologies of all public education. They therefore have decided that the only way to protect their children from indoctrination in religious beliefs of Humanism is to reject the public school system. They seek Chris-

---

1 John W. Whitehead. *The Second American Revolution* (Elgin, IL: David C. Cook publishers, 1982), 104.
2 For a more thorough discussion of legal changes to the definition of religion, read John W. Whitehead, *The Second American Revolution,* 104–108.
3 (20 367 U.S. 488 [1961] footnote 11).
4 Among them are *Washington Ethical Society v. District of Columbia,* 101 U.S. Appellate D.C. 371, 249 F 2nd 127 (1957); *Fellowship of Humanity v. County of Alameda,* 153 Cal. App. 2nd 673, 315 P. 2nd 394 (1957); *Jaffree v. Board of School Commissioners of Mobile County,* 554 F. Supp. 1104, 1129 n. 41 (1983); *Zorach v. Clauson,* 343 U.S. 306, 314 (1952).

tian educational alternatives—often home-schooling their own children.

One of the goals of the American Humanist Association is to place a Humanist counselor in every public school in America.

Humanism Acts Like a Religion

Humanism promotes values that seek to change lives, to worship mankind, and to have religious assumptions.

Humanism Seeks to Change Lives

A publication of the American Humanist Association states: "The American Humanist Association is a non-profit organization, funded in the early 1940s to provide an alternative religious philosophy."[5] The AHA seeks "people interested in becoming certified Humanist Leaders, Counselors, or ordained Ministers." "A Humanist Counselor, AHA, is the legal equivalent of minister, priest, rabbi . . . Humanist counselors, AHA, may act as chaplains on campuses and in prisons, hospitals, and other institutions where the presence of a non-traditional or non-theistic minister is often a need."[6] "To extend its principles and operate educationally, the Association publishes books, magazines, and pamphlets; engages lecturers; selects, trains and accredits Humanist Counselors as its ordained ministry of the movement . . ."[7]

One of the goals of the American Humanist Association is to place a Humanist counselor in every public school in America.[8] If that effort is successful, Humanist counselors will be able to give

---

5 As quoted by Lottie Beth Hobbs, "Humanist Ministers and Counselors," *Pro-Family Forum Alert* (Ft. Worth, TX: September, 1984), 3.
6 Ibid.
7 *Bylaws of the American Humanist Association*, "Preamble," 2.
8 Hobbs, 3.

guidance freely, according to principles of Humanism, to children of Christian parents without their parents ever knowing of it.

Humanism Worships Mankind

Christians are rightly concerned that Humanism is recognized as religion, and that, as religion, it is currently being taught in all public schools. However, the primary concern of Christians is not its being labeled as a religion. Rather, it is that Humanism is a form of self-worship.

Although the term *Humanism* became popular only in the last quarter of the twentieth century, its concepts have existed as long as mankind has existed. Eve was the first Humanist. She wanted to become like God by eating the forbidden fruit (Genesis 3:5–6). Those who started to build the Tower of Babel wanted to make for themselves a great name. Their intent was to build a tower with "its top in the heavens" (Genesis 11:4–7). This was probably an assertion of their independence from God. Throughout history, men have considered themselves gods. Tyre was destroyed because its proud heart declared, "I am God" (Ezekiel 28:2). The paramount worship of mankind throughout history has been that of self-worship.[1]

Humanism is a form of self-worship.

Humanity Study Versus Humanity Worship

Secular Humanism differs considerably from that of Renaissance Humanism. Renaissance humanists were students of the humanities. In reading ancient, non-Christian documents of hu-

---

1 Herbert Schlossberg, *Idols for Destruction: Christian Faith and Its Confrontation with American Society* (Nashville: Thomas Nelson Publishers, 1983), 40, quoting Arnold Toynbee, Reconsiderations, vol. 12 of *A Study of History* (New York: Oxford Univ. Press, 1961), 488.

manity, humanists absorbed many pagan assumptions regarding the nature of man. Subsequently, they began rejecting Christian perspectives. Humanism gradually changed from being primarily a study of the humanities to becoming the worship of humanity.

In the nineteenth century, French philosopher August Comte established a formal Religion of Humanity for the worship of all mankind—past, present, and future.

> This religion had a catechism, sacraments, a sacred calendar, a priesthood, prayers and something imitative of the Trinity. It also had a social system of which Comte was the chief planner. The Religion of Humanity, as a visible institution, for a time had great vitality. Comteans formed positivist societies for the worship of great people, and their churches spread even to South Africa.[2]

After the death of Comte, the formal designation of the "Religion of Humanity" gradually changed to "Humanism." Since then, the informal worship of humanity has continued to grow.

Society of Self

Humanism produces self-worship in many forms, and even though Christian faith recognizes self, it calls for self-denial and selflessness. However, Humanism promotes self-esteem, self-integration, self-determination, and self-actualization—ideals that have produced a very selfish society. Selfishness seeks hedonistic lifestyles through homosexuality, pornography, gambling, drug abuse, and the like. Selfishness produces divorce and is the primary motivation for abortion. In our society, selfishness has become a virtue. Many books about the wisdom of looking out for "number one" are bestsellers.

Selfishness is the logical result of a religion that promotes man as his own god.

---

2 Schlossberg, 41.

Although Humanists generally do not designate humanity by titles of deity, their language ascribes to man the roles and attributes of God. Humanism implies that man is all-powerful, all-wise, and sovereign (autonomous)—that he is his own savior and the only lawgiver. Humanism must reject any law or moral code that is not derived from human wisdom. That includes the Bible!

Contrasting Religious Worldviews

Humanists cannot prove God does not exist, or that he does not intervene in human events. They assume man has no spiritual nature, is self-existing, and that all things evolve. They assume there are no absolute moral values, ethics is autonomous, and man is not accountable to God after this life. Humanism assumes there is no sin and therefore no need for eternal salvation. Humanism assumes there is no life after death—no heaven or hell.

The religions of Christianity and Humanism conflict in many ways, only a few of which are noted here. As other categories are presented, other religious conflicts will be noted.

Religious Foundations

Christianity is a philosophical and historical religion based on the person and work of Jesus Christ and divine revelation. Humanism claims to be "a philosophical, religious, and moral point of view."[1] Humanism is a religion based on naturalism, rationalism, and scientism. Whereas Christians believe God alone authorizes what mankind should believe and do, Humanists believe only mankind should formulate a religion relevant to this age.[2]

Existence and Relevancy of God

Christians believe God is existent and relevant, being philosophically the first cause of all effects, who functions as creator, provider, lawgiver, judge, redeemer, and lord. They also believe God is faithful, omnipotent, sovereign, omniscient, omnipresent, per-

---

1 *Humanist Manifestoes I & II*, Preface.
2 *Humanist Manifesto I*, Introduction, paragraph 2.

sonal, holy, and true. On the other hand, Humanists believe God is non-existent and not relevant, that he is a mythological character—the product of human imagination—like an elf or leprechaun. Humanism is atheistic by its very nature.

Understanding of Nature
Christians believe the universe was created by God and is temporal. Humanists believe the universe is self-existing and therefore eternal. Christians think all creatures were designed, remain constant, and reproduce after their own kind; Humanists think all living things have evolved by chance and continue in an upward progression.

Humanity
Christians believe mankind has both physical and spiritual natures, is a free moral agent, and was created by God in his own image. Humanists believe mankind has only a physical nature, is only temporal, and is basically good, being the highest form of evolutionary development. Christians believe that although mankind is the best of God's creation, everyone is a sinner needing salvation from sin and guidance from God. Humanists believe human beings are self-sufficient, able to govern themselves, and apart from God are able to save themselves from their problems. Christians think all people have limited authority, are accountable to God, and have an eternal destiny. Humanists believe humans constitute supreme authority and are therefore accountable only to themselves. Humanists deny the possibility of any eternal destiny. Christians think belief in God is not only realistic (i.e., sane) but that it is foolish not to believe in God (Psalm 14:1; 53:1). Humanists think belief in God is unrealistic (i.e., insane).[3]

---

3 "We assume that Humanism will take the path of social and mental hygiene and discourage sentimental and unreal hopes and wishful thinking." *Humanist Manifesto I*, Eleven.

CHRISTIANITY OR HUMANISM

The Source and Nature of Religion

Christians perceive reality to be physical, spiritual, and eternal, comprising both natural and supernatural realms. They believe religion must be established and presented by God. Humanists perceive reality to be only physical and temporal, consisting of only the natural realm. They believe religion must be established and maintained only by human reasoning and scientific methodology. Christians believe reality must be ascertained by both natural and divine revelation. Humanists believe reality can be ascertained only by natural revelation. While Christianity requires that knowledge be obtained by the word of God, Humanism requires free inquiry (i.e., being unhampered by divine revelation) in its quest for knowledge.

Christianity produces human submission to divine revelation and reverence toward God. Humanism produces maximum individual autonomy.

Immortality

Christians believe every soul has an eternal destiny; Humanists deny that people have souls.[1] Christians think obedient believers go to heaven and unrepentant sinners go to hell, but Humanists deny any eternal destiny of individuals either in heaven or hell.[2] The Christian religion seeks salvation from sin, holiness in this life, and eternal life with God rather than eternal punishment with Satan. The religion of Humanism seeks complete realization of the human personality and the good life in the here and now.[3] Christians believe people are sinners, needing salvation from sin, and by obedient faith in Jesus Christ, sinners receive God's grace

---

1 "Modern science discredits such historic concepts as the "ghost in the machine" and the "separable soul." *Humanist Manifesto II*, Second.
2 "There is no credible evidence that life survives the death of the body." Ibid.
3 *Humanist Manifesto II*, Third.

of salvation. Humanists on the other hand presume humanity is basically good (i.e., not sinners); the only salvation needed is from their temporal problems.[4]

Regarding perspectives on immortality, Christians believe Humanism unrealistically rejects the supernatural, leaving humanity without God, unprepared for eternal judgment. Humanists believe traditional religions (such as Christianity) do a disservice to humanity.[5] They consider belief in immortal salvation both illusory and harmful.[6]

RELIGION	Biblical Christianity	or	Secular Humanism
Foundation	Based on person and work of Jesus Christ; from divine authority	or	Based on naturalism, rationalism, scientism; from human authority
Existence of God	God is considered creator, provider, holy, true, redeemer all-wise.	or	God is considered non-existent and non-relevant; a mythological person
Nature	Created by God	or	Evolved by chance
Humanity	Physical and spiritual; dependent on God	or	Only physical; but self-sufficient
Source of Religion	God	or	Human reasoning
Immortality	Eternal life	or	No afterlife
SUMMARY	God	or	Man

---

4 "They believe that men and women are free and are responsible for their own destinies and that they cannot look toward some transcendent Being for salvation." *A Secular Humanist Declaration*, 6. "What more pressing need than to recognize in this critical age of modern science and technology that, if no deity will save us, we must save ourselves? It is only by assuming responsibility for the human condition and in marshaling the arts of intelligence that humankind can hope to deal with the emerging problems of the twenty-first century and beyond." *Humanist Manifestos I & II*, Preface.
5 *Humanist Manifesto II*, First.
6 *Humanist Manifesto II*, Second.

Why Christianity Is Superior to Humanism

Proof that Christianity is superior to Humanism is much more abundant than the two fundamental reasons presented below. Other reasons may be inferred when examining additional areas of life.

Consistency

The Christian religion is consistent with Christian declarations; Humanist theology is not consistent with Humanist declarations. Because Christians can demonstrate the validity of their beliefs from both natural and divine revelation, the Christian religion is consistent with Christian declarations. On the other hand, Humanists cannot prove their beliefs either by natural science or by reason. Here are a few examples of their unproved tenets.

Humanists cannot prove these contentions:
- There is no God.
- Matter is eternal.
- All things originated through evolution.
- Man is only physical.
- Man has no demonstrative purpose in life.

Although Humanists claim their religion must be established by scientific methodology,[1] their religion is not scientifically provable.

Identity

Christianity gives better answers to questions of identity. Like all other religions, Humanism seeks to answer basic and ultimate questions regarding reality. To the question, "Who am I?" Humanists answer that "man is a part of nature and that he has emerged

---

1 "Religion must formulate its hopes and plans in the light of the scientific spirit and method." *Humanist Manifesto I*, Fifth.

as the result of a continuous process."[2] On the other hand, to the question, "Who am I?" Christians answer that everyone is more than an animal (Genesis 9:2–3, 6), although just a little lower than angels (Psalm 8:5; Hebrews 2:7, 9). Even so, all are children of God by creation (Genesis 3:20; Acts 17:26), while some are also special children of God by redemption in Christ Jesus (John 1:12–13; Galatians 3:26).

IDENTITY	Biblical Christianity	or	Secular Humanism
Who Am I?	Child of God	or	Product of nature
Where Did I Come From?	Created by God	or	Evolved by chance
Why Am I Here?	To glorify and serve God; to serve others	or	No purpose; just here by accident
Where Am I Going?	Eternity destiny—life or death	or	Nowhere—life's fulfillment is only here and now
How Do I Get There?	By God's grace and my faithful service	or	By personal achievements
SUMMARY	God	or	Man

To the question, "Where did I come from?" Humanists respond that "the human species is an emergence from natural evolutionary forces."[3] Christians answer that mankind was created by God: made from the dust of the ground and in the image of God (Genesis 2:7; 3:19; 1:26–27; 9:6). Man is therefore both physical and spiritual in nature.

To the question, "Why am I here?" Humanism declares, "The ultimate goal should be the fulfillment of the potential for growth in each human personality—not for the favored few, but for all of humankind."[4] "Commitment to all humankind is the highest commitment of which we are capable; it transcends the narrow allegiances of church, state, party, class, or race in moving toward a wider vision of human potentiality."[5]

---

2 *Humanist Manifesto I*, Second.
3 *Humanist Manifesto II*, Second.
4 *Humanist Manifesto II*, Preface.
5 *Humanist Manifesto II*, In closing.

To that same question, "Why am I here?" Christians answer that man is made to glorify God and to serve God and humanity (Matthew 25:21, 23; 1 Thessalonians 1:9; Hebrews 11:28; 1 Corinthians 9:19; Galatians 5:13).

To the question, "Where am I going?" Humanists answer, "Religious Humanism considers the complete realization of human personality to be the end of man's life and seeks its development and fulfillment in the here and now."[1]

Christians answer the question, "Where am I going?" by saying that everyone has an eternal destiny (John 5:28–29; Romans 6:23; 2 Thessalonians 1:7–9). After death man will be resurrected to face God in judgment (Ecclesiastes 11:9; 12:14; Acts 17:30–31; Hebrews 9:27). Depending upon an individual's beliefs and conduct, he or she will be rewarded either with eternal life with God in heaven or condemned with eternal punishment with Satan in hell (Matthew 25:31–46).

To the question, "How do I get there?" Humanists respond, "Believing that religion must work increasingly for joy in human living, religious Humanists aim to foster the creative in man and to encourage achievements that add to the satisfaction of life."[2]

On the other hand, to the question, "How do I get there?" Christians respond that a life of faith and service is essential to receive eternal life, and unbelief will result in everlasting punishment.

Logical Thinking

Which is better: Thinking God's design and purpose are the cause of human ancestry or thinking humans evolved by blind chance? A belief in God's purposes gives meaning to life; a belief in life from non-life negates meaningful life. Thinking humanity (being both physical and spiritual, both temporal and immortal) is superior to animals (being only physical and temporal) is surely better than thinking humanity is only like animals. Believing life is best lived when spent in praise to God and service to mankind is

---

1 *Humanist Manifesto I*, Eighth.
2 *Humanist Manifesto II*, Twelfth.

surely better than believing life is to be spent in selfish, materialistic, and hedonistic pursuits. To live with belief in an eternal reward for having lived a good life in faithful service to both God and man is surely better than to think death / annihilation is the inescapable end.

Christian answers to these questions of identity are better than Humanist answers for reasons both temporal and eternal. Humanist answers result in ultimate absolute nothingness and eternal condemnation; Christian answers result in meaningfulness and eternal life.

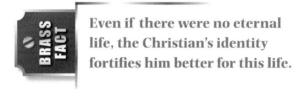

Even if there were no eternal life, the Christian's identity fortifies him better for this life.

Conclusion

Humanism may be recognized as a religion because it claims to be a religion, it has been legally declared to be a religion, and it acts like a religion. Humanists seek to change lives, worship mankind, and make religious assumptions. Christians and Humanists differ in their religious foundations and in their beliefs about immortality. Their beliefs differ regarding the existence and relevancy of God. Their understandings also differ regarding nature, humanity, and the source and nature of religion.

Two reasons may be given to support the contention that the Christian religion is superior to the religion of Humanism.

- The Christian religion is consistent with Christian beliefs, but Humanist theology is not consistent with the tenets of Humanism.

- The Christian religion gives better answers to questions of identity than does the religion of secular Humanism.

Much . . . may be said of the Court's interpretation of the religion clauses of the First Amendment. The liberal intelligentsia is overwhelmingly secular and fearful of religion, hence its incessant harping on the dangers posed by the "religious right." That ominous phrase is intended to suggest that Americans who are conservative and religious are a threat to the Republic, for they are probably intending to establish a theocracy and to institute an ecumenical version of the Inquisition. (Exasperated, a friend suggested that the press should begin referring to the "pagan left.") It is certainly true, however, that the liberal intelligentsia's antagonism to religion is now a prominent feature of American jurisprudence. The Court moved rather suddenly from tolerance of religion and religious expression to fierce hostility.[1]

—Robert H. Bork

PLAYING WITH FIRE

Abby cried to her mother, "I don't understand my homework!" Third grade was so different from last year. In class the next day, when Ms. Sisk asked, "What is two times two?" Abby answered, "Six."

"Six is a good answer," Ms. Sisk responded. "But four is the better answer."

What are the consequences when Humanism promotes self-esteem above truth?

---

1 Coercing Virtue: The Worldwide Rule of Judges (Washington, D.C.: The AEI Press, 2003), 65.

RELIGION

Review Questions

1. Present evidence that proves Humanism is a religion.
2. In what ways does Humanism act like a religion?
3. List some assumptions of the religion of Humanism?
4. What is the religious foundation of Christianity?
5. What is the religious foundation of Humanism?
6. How do Christians and Humanists differ in their view of God?
7. How do Christians and Humanists differ in their views regarding the origin of the universe?
8. How do Christians and Humanists differ in their views regarding the nature of humanity?
9. How do Christians and Humanists differ in their views regarding the establishment of religion?
10. How do Christians and Humanists differ in their views regarding immortality?
11. In what ways is the Christian religion superior to the religion of Humanism?
12. How do Christians and Humanists answer differently the major questions of identity?
13. What are some important implications derived from recognizing the fact that Humanism is a religion?

CHAPTER

PHILOSOPHY

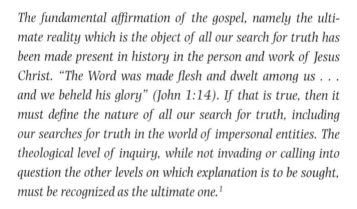

The fundamental affirmation of the gospel, namely the ultimate reality which is the object of all our search for truth has been made present in history in the person and work of Jesus Christ. "The Word was made flesh and dwelt among us . . . and we beheld his glory" (John 1:14). If that is true, then it must define the nature of all our search for truth, including our searches for truth in the world of impersonal entities. The theological level of inquiry, while not invading or calling into question the other levels on which explanation is to be sought, must be recognized as the ultimate one.[1]

Everyone has a philosophy of life, whether or not he readily acknowledges it. *Philosophy* is a compound of two Greek words, *philo* meaning love, and *sophia* meaning wisdom or knowledge. So by definition, a philosopher is one who loves knowledge or wisdom. The word *philosophy* is frequently used to describe one's worldview or outlook on life. As a discipline, philosophy may be categorized as natural, moral, and metaphysical. What follows relates to metaphysical philosophy.

---

1 Lesslie Newbign, *Proper Confidence: Faith, Doubt & Certainty in Christian Discipleship* (Grand Rapids: William B. Eerdmans Publishing Company, 1995), 63.

According to Webster, metaphysical philosophy "deals with first principles and seeks to explain the nature of being or reality (ontology) and of the origin and structure of the world (cosmology): it is closely associated with a theory of knowledge (epistemology)." Since *metaphysics, ontology, cosmology,* and *epistemology* are words not commonly used in popular conversation, they may be new to some readers. However, readers need to understand these terms. Christians and Humanists differ in their metaphysical worldviews. These differences can be contrasted categorically and then arguments can be presented to demonstrate that the Christian philosophical worldview is superior to that of Humanism.

Contrasting Philosophical Worldviews

Epistemology (theory of knowledge)

For Christians, acquisition of knowledge is based on natural and divine revelation. Because they accept divine revelation, as well as truths revealed through nature, experience, and history, Christians believe in the existence of God, in spiritual truths as revealed in the Bible, and in eternal realities. On the other hand, Humanists believe acquisition of knowledge is based only on natural revelation. Humanists limit their epistemology to whatever can be known by naturalism, materialism, rationalism, and scientism.

- *Naturalism* is the belief that nature is all there is. Hence, no knowledge may be obtained from any presumed divine revelation.

- *Materialism*, an extension of naturalism, is the belief that matter is all there is—no spiritual nature exists.

- *Rationalism* is the belief that only human reason is needed to ascertain truth. Hence, no presumed divine guidance or proclamations are allowed.

- *Scientism* is the belief that the scientific method is sufficient for ascertaining all truth, whether of physical and biological sciences or of other disciplines, such as the humanities and the social sciences. Whatever cannot be ascertained by the scientific method (i.e., through the senses of sight, sound, smell, touch, and taste) or human reasoning cannot be said to exist.

Through these limitations imposed by naturalism, materialism, rationalism, and scientism, Humanists reject the existence of God, spiritual truths as revealed in the Bible, and eternal realities.

For Christians, knowledge is derived from both natural and divine revelation, but for Humanists, knowledge is derived only from natural revelation.

Ontology (nature of being)

Ontology is concerned first with whether or not God exists. For Christians, ontological arguments for the existence of God come from reason, natural science, and divine revelation.

Reason

Christians affirm God's existence by arguing from what may be called "mental proof," and by presenting the ontological and teleological arguments. The supernaturalist may argue that one's ability to think cannot be considered a physical, material thing. While the brain is physical, the mind is not. It is of another nature. If the mind is not physical, then the only rational option is to believe there must have been an Ultimate Mind to bring it into existence.

This "mental proof" prepares the way for accepting three major philosophical arguments for the existence of God.

- *The Teleological Argument*: since there is design in the physical universe, a cosmic Designer and Creator must exist.

- *The Ontological Argument*: the perfect being, as conceived by mankind, must actually exist because human beings cannot conceive of that which does not exist. This argument, first stated by Anselm (A.D.1033–1109), weds two concepts together. The first is that God is a "being than which nothing greater can be conceived." The second is that something that exists only in the mind is distinct from what exists in mind and reality. Because it is impossible to conceive of a more perfect being than the most perfect being, then God must exist in reality, not just in mind.

- *The Cosmological Argument* distinguishes between necessary and contingent beings, and asserts that God is the necessary being which explains the existence of all other (i.e., contingent) beings.

DOES GOD EXIST?	Biblical Christianity	or	Secular Humanism
Teleological argument	Design in nature demands that there be a designer.	or	Apparent designs in nature evolved by random chance.
Ontological argument	Since people conceive of a perfect being (i.e., God), and since humans cannot conceive of that which does not exist, then God exists!	or	God is but a figment of man's imagination, created in man's own image.
Cosmological argument	God is the necessary being which explains the existence of all other, i.e., contingent beings.	or	There was no beginning; the universe is self-existing—eternal.
SUMMARY	Natural science, reason, divine revelation, and the dualistic nature of mankind all argue for the existence of God.	or	Only matter exists. The supernatural and the spiritual are considered as unreal.

Natural Science

From natural science, Christians argue the existence of God from the second law of thermodynamics, the impossibility of spontaneous generation, DNA genetic information, and the Anthropic Principle.

1. *The second law of thermodynamics* indicates that everything is naturally deteriorating, not improving; therefore a supernatural Creator must have made everything better than it now is.

PHILOSOPHY

2. *The impossibility of life coming from non-life* means there must be a supernatural life to have produced life on earth.

3. *The DNA genetic code,* which prohibits life forms from moving from one type of organism into another, requires that a supernatural Codifier must have given each life form its specific genetic code.

4. *The Anthropic Principle* declares that the parameters of the earth were specifically tailored for life on earth—for example, the earth is just the right distance from the sun, being neither too hot nor too cold—and argues that a supernatural power had to arrange these conditions.

Divine Revelation

Christians may also cite philosophical arguments for the existence of God from Scripture. For example, some characteristics of Christian philosophy are given in John 1:1–4:

- Mind before matter
- God before man
- Plan and design before creation
- Life from life
- Enlightenment from the Light[1]

The Christian philosophy is also affirmed from Scripture by an abundance of other evidence—for example, fulfilled prophecies, accuracy in recorded historical data, and pre-scientific declarations of true facts about the universe.

Christian arguments affirming the existence of God are derived from reason, natural science, philosophy, and Scripture.

---

1 This example comes from David Noebel, *Understanding the Times: The Story of the Biblical Christian, Marxist/Leninist and Secular Humanist Worldviews* (Manitou Springs, CO: Summit Press, 1991), 166–167.

CHRISTIANITY OR HUMANISM

In spite of these arguments, Humanist ontology requires a denial of the existence of God. Since Humanists contend that nature is all there is, for them there can be no supernatural. Since they contend that matter is all there is, for them there can be nothing spiritual. Since they contend that truth is ascertainable only by human reasoning, there can be no divine revelation; beliefs based on supernatural revelation are invalid. Humanist ontology is thus limited by its epistemology.

Cosmology (origin and structure of the world)
Because cosmology deals with the origin of the world, it entertains the possibility of either creation or evolution. If the earth was created, then the argument must relate to the existence of God. Because cosmology deals with the structure of the world, it recognizes the possibility of God's intervention in history in various ways, with the nature of man, and such like. In cosmology, like ontology, Christians argue from both reason and revelation; Humanists argue only from reasoning that is limited by their epistemology.

Regarding the existence of God, the Cosmological Argument distinguishes between necessary beings and dependent beings; it asserts that God is the necessary being who explains the existence of people and all other contingent beings. God, therefore, is the First Cause of all causes. Humanists reject the idea of First Cause because they believe there was no beginning. They believe the universe is self-existing—eternal.

Christians and Humanists conflict regarding the origin of the universe. Was it created or did it evolve? Because Humanists reject the existence of God on ontological grounds, the universe simply could not have been created. It had to evolve!

Humanists reject the existence of God, so they must reject all notions that God has anything to do with human events. For Humanists, God could not have been involved in Noah's worldwide flood. God could not have led the Israelites out of Egypt, nor could He have been interactive with the judges and kings of Israel and Judah. Surely He had nothing to do with the Babylonian captivity

PHILOSOPHY

of the Jews; neither could He have had any connection with the life and teachings of Jesus. God could have had nothing to do with the establishment of the church or with the ongoing lives of Christians.

For Humanists, there can be no such thing as a miracle. God can have nothing to do with natural catastrophes such as droughts, tornadoes, or hurricanes. For them, God does not punish individuals or nations for their sins or reward them for their faithfulness to him. The Humanists' stance regarding God's interaction with humanity quite obviously conflicts with Christian faith.

Regarding the nature of man, Christians contend that mankind is dualistic—both physical and spiritual. Humanists contend that mankind is monistic—only physical. Humanists reject the Christian belief that upon death the physical body goes back to the ground but the spiritual body goes to God for judgment. Humanists reject Christian beliefs of eternal destiny in heaven or hell.

Why Christian Philosophy Is Superior

Perception of Knowledge

Christian philosophy is consistent with its perception of how things can be known. Humanist philosophy is inconsistent with its manner of acquiring knowledge. Christian philosophy receives, from both natural and supernatural sources, abundant supporting evidence that affirms Christian philosophy and negates Humanist philosophy. Humanists inconsistently reject arguments and evidences from reason and natural sciences that affirm Christian beliefs, simply because such do not fit their epistemology.

Reasonability

Christian philosophy is more reasonable than Humanist philosophy. The Teleological Argument, the Ontological Argument, and the Cosmological Argument are based on reason. They support the existence of God. Evidences for biblical faith, supported by divine revelation, fulfilled prophecies, archaeology, and history are more reasonable than Humanist faith, which is limited by its epistemology.

Consistent with Natural Sciences

Christian philosophy is more consistent with the natural sciences. Since Humanist philosophy declares that nature is all there is and that knowledge can be obtained only through the scientific method, then Humanists must demonstrate through nature that knowledge can be obtained only by the scientific method. But natural science cannot disprove the existence of God, nor does the scientific method demonstrate that knowledge can be obtained only through the scientific method. None of these Humanist assumptions—nature is all there is, beliefs can be determined only by the scientific method, God does not exist, the universe is self-existing, the theory of evolution is true, man is monistic, and man may acquire knowledge only through reasoning—are provable by the scientific method! Humanists are inconsistent.

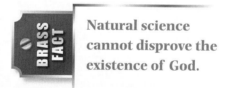

BRASS FACT: Natural science cannot disprove the existence of God.

Christians should not lose sight of the fact that modern science developed because people came to believe the Christian perspective that this world has order. People can test and verify their ideas only if experiments are repeatable. If this world were a place where all things happen by chance, then science itself could never have developed. Christians may counter Humanism by using science and nature in two ways: first, by showing that evidences from natural sciences often contradict Humanist beliefs, and second, by demonstrating that design and order exist in the universe (as opposed to the Humanist assumption that all things operate by chance). Humanists can maintain their position only by turning a blind eye to natural and scientific evidences that support Christian beliefs and oppose Humanist beliefs.

Conclusion

Christian philosophy is supported by teleological, ontological and cosmological arguments. It denies naturalism, yet employs natural science. It denies rationalism, yet uses reasoning. It denies scientism, yet accepts the scientific method. It also relies upon divine revelation. Christian philosophy is superior to Humanist philosophy, not only because it offers a better explanation of reality, but also because it alone provides explanations that correspond to reality. Its epistemology is consistent with both natural and supernatural revelation; its arguments are supported by reasoning; and its conclusions are consistent with genuine findings in the natural sciences.

In our day, humanistic reason affirms that there is only the cosmic machine, which encompasses everything, including people. To those who hold this view everything people are or do is explained by some form of determinism, some type of behaviorism, some kind of reductionism. The terms *determinism* or *behaviorism* indicate that everything people think or do is determined in a machine-like way and that any sense of freedom or choice is an illusion. In one form of reductionism, man is explained by reducing him to the smallest particles which make up his body. Man is seen as being only the molecule or the energy particle, more complex but not intrinsically different.[1]

---

1 Francis A. Schaeffer, *How Should We Then Live? The Rise and Decline of Western Thought and Culture* (Old Tappan, NJ: Fleming H. Revell Company, 1976), 164.

CHRISTIANITY OR HUMANISM

PLAYING WITH FIRE

Jeremy's professor speaks with disdain about Christianity; no student dares to defy this teacher! Not only does Jeremy feel doubts about Mr. Glynn's philosophy, he also has begun to doubt Christian teachings. He realizes that if he accepts the belief that the Bible is *not* divine truth, then he must recognize Jesus Christ as the greatest liar of all time. Jeremy is miserable as he reads the following Bible verses:

> As you have therefore received Christ Jesus the Lord, so walk in Him, rooted and built up in Him and established in the faith, as you have been taught, abounding in it with thanksgiving. Beware lest anyone cheat you through philosophy and empty deceit, according to the tradition of men, according to the basic principles of the world, and not according to Christ. For in Him dwells all the fullness of the Godhead bodily; and you are complete in Him, who is the head of all principality and power (Colossians 2:6–10).

Which phrase from this Scripture do you think disturbs Jeremy most?

Review Questions

1. Define the following terms: epistemology, ontology, cosmology, teleology, naturalism, materialism, rationalism, scientism.

2. What is meant by the following expressions? The *second law of thermodynamics*, spontaneous generation, the Anthropic Principle, and the dualistic view of man.

3. What is the Ontological Argument for the existence of God?

4. What is the Teleological Argument for the existence of God?

5. What is the Cosmological Argument for the existence of God?

6. Give an example of how special revelation argues for the existence of God.

7. How do Christians and Humanists differ in their epistemology?

8. How do Christians and Humanists differ in their ontology?

9. How do Christians and Humanists differ in their cosmology?

10. In what ways is Christian philosophy superior to Humanist philosophy?

11. How will an understanding of these philosophical terms and arguments enable you to respond better to Humanism?

Suggested Reading in Philosophy

Sire, James W. *The Universe Next Door*, Downers Grove, IL: InterVarsity Press, 2004.

CHAPTER

HISTORY

Whether time is important or unimportant, intelligible or absurd, cyclical or linear are questions intimately bound up with the most fundamental of metaphysical, anthropological, and theological convictions. The linearity of Western conceptions of history reflects the conviction that history is what comes between creation and final judgment. But there are other models. Ancient histories of cyclical history were related to religious ideas concerning the periodic nature of redemption . . . What we think of the meaning of history is inseparable from what we think of the meaning of life . . . That the question of history has any importance at all is in itself a religious conclusion.[1]

History is a record of man's activities on earth. How one interprets history depends upon one's philosophy of history. Christians and Humanists differ regarding their understandings of history because their different basic philosophies or worldviews are shaped by their respective ideologies. The fundamental difference between the Christian and the Humanist worldview is that the Christian recognizes the existence of God, the spiritual nature of man, and relationships between God and mankind; the Humanist

---

1 Herbert Schlossberg, *Idols for Destruction: The Conflict of Christian Faith and American Culture* (Wheaton, IL: Crossway Books, 1990), 12.

does not. Here are other differences between Christian and Humanist concepts, followed by reasons Christian history is superior to Humanist history.

Contrasting Historical Worldviews

Origin of History

Christians believe history is time-bound and linear. It began with God's creation of the heavens and the earth, and it will end with the final judgment at the coming of Christ. Everyone will then receive a designation to an eternal destiny of either heaven or hell. Because human beings are both physical and spiritual, the physical aspect of life will cease, but the spiritual aspect of life will live on.

For Humanists history evolves from a self-existing universe. Humanists do not believe in life after death. They believe the only future of humanity is that of mankind in general, and that the future will be in a material universe.

Progression of History

Christians believe God is active in history. God has acted in human history through mighty acts, such as the biblical accounts of Creation, the Flood, the Tower at Babel, miracles in Israel's deliverance from Egypt and conquest of Canaan, the incarnation and resurrection of Christ—the list is endless. God answers prayer, rules over nations, and gives providential guidance to individuals. Christians realize that civilizations fail when the judgment of God is pronounced against them for their immorality. Being realistic about the moral nature of mankind, Christians realize there will be no moral improvement of humanity apart from acceptance of Christian moral principles. Christians believe history can be improved whenever individuals within societies improve their morality. Christians assess history based on discernment of the purpose of God in the world.

Humanists deny the reality of God and reject all suggestions that God acts within history. They optimistically believe civilizations will improve because their evolutionary worldview leads them to think humanity has progressed upward from simple to complex forms of life. They suggest that since such progress has happened, it will surely continue. Humanists believe progress is not guaranteed, however, because that would require a guarantor. Humanists assess history based on their rational system of ethics. For Humanists, historical groups are evaluated on their supposed contribution to the human good.

Christians believe God is active in history. Humanists reject the idea that God can be active in history because they deny the existence and relevancy of God.

Relationship of Cause and Effect in History

Christians believe God is the root cause of historical events. He created mankind, provided a moral standard for human behavior, and rules over human affairs. God's moral standard is the basis for measuring human activities. History results from human behavior and God's judgments upon it. Civilizations rise or fall based on God's judgment and on human conformity to God's moral order. The biblical worldview of history, determined by human morality in relation to God's will, grants a consistent basis for understanding human history. It gives purpose and meaning to a society's history. Christians believe that because human beings have free will, they are motivated to influence both individuals and the world at large to conform to God's moral and spiritual order. Christians seek individual and eternal salvation for themselves and others. Christians also seek to provide a Christian environment in which everyone may live in freedom. The Christian quest for conformity to God's moral order has shaped the direction of history since the time Christ lived on earth.

Humanists believe human ideologies shape the directions of history. The evolutionary belief that all things happen by random chance logically means history cannot be shaped by God. Nor will chance logically allow history to be shaped by the concept of human progress.

Some Humanists assert that human environment shapes history. But if human environment is all that shapes history, then people have no free will, are stripped of a purpose, and cannot be motivated to change the world. Therefore, many Humanists claim that human ideologies shape the directions of history. Although human ideologies are thought to evolve, some are considered more significant than others. Humanists consider that primitive and supernatural ideologies are insignificant. They think only Humanist ideologies provide humans with the ability to direct the course of history.

Jesus Christ

For Christians, Jesus is the central figure of all history. He is the Son of God who lived in the flesh and died on a cross to redeem people from their sins. Humanists perceive Jesus as having been only a good man among other good men. He could not have been the Son of God, Humanists think, because there is no God. In any event, for Humanists no one is a central person in history.

Accuracy of Biblical History

Christians believe the Bible reveals the only historical worldview that fits reality. The question of biblical accuracy is confirmed for Christians by the fact that the transmission of Scripture is judged to be extremely accurate.[1] Because they consider transmission of the biblical text to be accurate, Christians also consider the substance of biblical history to be accurate. However, Humanists

---

1 For scholarly statements about accuracy of the Bible, read David A. Noebel, *Understanding the Times, The Story of Biblical Christian, Marxist/Leninist and Secular Humanist Worldviews* (Manitou Springs, CO: Summit Press), 1991, 767–771.

HISTORY

consider the Bible inaccurate because atheistic theology and naturalistic philosophy forbid any considerations of biblical truthfulness.

BRASS FACT: Biblical history is considered by Humanists to be myth, legend, and allegory.

HISTORY	Biblical Christianity	or	Secular Humanism
Humanity	People are sinners in need of salvation.	or	Humanity can save itself.
Events	God is active in each life.	or	Humanity rules everything.
Origins	By creation	or	By evolution
Behavior	Restricted to God's requirements	or	Permitted to choose anything that is acceptable to society
SUMMARY	God	or	Man

Why Christian History Is Superior

Consistency in Ideology

Christian understanding is consistent with its ideology. Humanist understanding is inconsistent with its ideology. Christian understanding is consistent with its ideology because it realistically recognizes that the sinful nature of mankind produces civilizations that rise and fall. Humanist understanding is inconsistent with its ideology because its optimism about human progress in history is opposed to the evolutionary concept that all things happen by random chance. If all things happen by random chance, then the possibility of a negative future is the same as that of a positive one.

Consistency in Historical and Scientific Facts

The Bible, the basis of Christian understanding, concurs with actual historical and scientific facts. The theory of evolution, the basis of Humanist history, does not concur with actual historical and scientific facts. The question Christians must answer satisfactorily is: "Is the Bible historically accurate?" Since biblical archeology confirms accuracy in transmission of the biblical text, then Christians may appeal to data from biblical archeology to verify biblical history. Because archeology has never nullified a fact indicated by biblical history, biblical history can be presumed as accurate. The question that Humanists must answer satisfactorily is, "What certifies the accuracy of the theory of evolution?" Since the evidence for evolution is neither scientifically nor rationally superior to the evidence for creation, then a type of fideistic belief system is required of Humanists to accept it as true.

 In the U.S., only 14 percent of adults thought that evolution was "definitely true," while about a third firmly rejected the idea.[1]

Solid Basis for Assessment of the Future

Unlike Humanists, Christians have a solid basis for assessment of the future. Christians assess future possibilities on the same basis as they assess the past: God rules over history according to His own will. That will requires human behavior—individually and collectively—to conform to His moral standard as set forth in Scripture and exemplified by the life of Christ. When people conform to God's standard, their future is bright because God blesses them. But when people reject God and His will, their future is dreary because God turns away from them.

This concept is declared in Deuteronomy 28, as well as in many other places in Scripture. This concept is also demonstrated in biblical history. Christians may therefore assess future possibilities of individuals and societies by whether or not they are abiding by the will of God and conforming to His moral standards. Those

---

1 *National Geographic News*, August 10, 2006. http://news.nationalgeographic.com/news/2006/08/060810-evolution.html

HISTORY

who assess their individual lives by Christian standards may recognize whether they will ultimately go to heaven or hell. Those who assess their societies by God's standards may realize whether their societies will survive because of righteousness or be doomed because of wickedness.

While Humanists are generally optimistic about their future, they have no solid basis for assessing the future of either individuals or societies because evolution is a philosophy that depends on random chance, and thus cannot guarantee progress. Even so, Humanists are generally optimistic about their future because the progress of mankind is the basis of Humanists hope. It is the only meaningful goal of Humanists.

 Random chance in the theory of evolution leaves human will without direction or guidance.

Conclusion

The biblical view of history is one of human redemption; that is, it recognizes that people are sinners and are in need of salvation. This view of history recognizes the activity of God in directing human events toward human redemption. The Christian view of history is significant, not only for its beginning (creation) and its ending (eschatology) but also for God's many events relating to human redemption, focused principally upon the person and work of Jesus Christ. The Christian worldview of history demands that human ethical behavior conform to God's requirements for salvation.

The Humanist view of history is one of humanity saving itself from whatever problems may evolve. This view of history rejects God and thrusts mankind into rulership over all human conditions. The Humanist view of history results in people's behaving as though there is no God and therefore no eternal judgment. The Humanist view of history allows people to conduct themselves in whatever way they choose, restricted by nothing other than whatever is considered acceptable by their society.

Christians view history through the concepts of creation, fall, and redemption, a progression of events beginning with God's good creation, humanity's rebellion against God, and God's ultimate plan for divine intervention, redemption, and restoration. Thus, all of creation is sacred and stands under the blessing, judging, and redeeming purposes of God. This belief of creation/fall/redemption/restoration has vast ramifications for humanity. If the Christian philosophy of history is correct, then not only is the overall story of humanity invested with meaning, but every moment that we live is charged with purpose.[1]

PLAYING WITH FIRE

At the end of her first quarter at the university, Lenora came home and announced: "I am not going to church anymore!"

Her parents were shocked. "Lenora, what happened?" wailed Mom. "You have all those awards for perfect attendance! And you've always seemed glad to worship God."

"I no longer believe in God; he is a myth," she replied bluntly. "Dr. Phillips has taught me the truth."

"How did Dr. Phillips teach you that God is a myth?" asked her dad.

"It really wasn't hard. He pointed out that apples do not grow in the Tigris-Euphrates Valley."

"Well?" Lenora's father was inquisitive.

"Dad." Lenora was impatient. "That being true, the first story in the Bible, the creation story, is a myth. The Garden of Eden was in the Tigris-Euphrates Valley, so Eve could not have eaten an apple as the Bible says. And if that story is a myth, why not all the others?"

---

1 David Noebel, *Understanding the Times: The Collision of Today's Competing Worldviews* (Manitou Springs, CO: Summit Press, 2006), 395.

HISTORY

"Hold on a minute, Lenora. Let's answer three questions. First, do we know the location of the Garden of Eden? No. Second, do we know the nature of the climate in the Garden? No. And third, what kind of fruit was forbidden? The Bible does not say. The myth here is the apple. Did Dr. Phillips read the Scripture?"

Lenora shrugged her shoulders and walked away. To Lenora, her dad was a good, old-fashioned man. Dr. Phillips was her authority. Facts no longer mattered to her. She had decided that all truth is relative, and what she had come to believe was right for her. Nothing else mattered.

Why does the Humanist view of history discount any logical point toward the existence of a Higher Being?

Review Questions

1. How do the Christian and Humanist ideas of history differ philosophically?

2. How do Christians and Humanists differ in their assessments of history?

3. How do Christians and Humanists differ in their philosophical understandings about the progression of history?

4. How do Christian and Humanist ideologies result in producing different perspectives about the causes and effects of history?

5. How do Christians and Humanists differ in their understandings of biblical history?

6. How do Christians and Humanists differ in their understandings of the nature and significance of Jesus Christ?

7. What are the results of understanding history from a Christian perspective, as opposed to understanding history from a Humanist perspective?

8. How may Christian thinking about history be considered superior to thinking about history from a Humanist perspective?

9. How is the Christian worldview of history significant to you?

CHAPTER

ETHICS

The fundamental question of ethics is, who makes the rules? God or men? The theistic answer is that God makes them. The humanist answer is that men make them. This distinction between theism and Humanism is the fundamental division in moral theory.[1]

Ethics is the study of morality. While technical distinctions exist between *ethics* and *morals*, the two terms are sometimes used interchangeably. Ethical differences between Christian and Humanist worldviews relate to their foundations, requirements, and characteristics. After these differences are described, arguments will follow that demonstrate why Christian ethics is superior to Humanist ethics.

Contrasting Ethical Worldviews

Ethical Foundations

Christian ethics comes from the character of God as revealed in the Bible. Christian ethics is apart from, but imposed upon, human beings, both individually and collectively. Many implications are derived from the fact that Christian ethics is theological.

---

1 Max Hocutt, "Toward an Ethic of Mutual Accommodation," in *Humanist Ethics*, ed. Morris B. Storer (Buffulo: Prometheus Books, 1980), 137.

- Christian ethics is an expansion of a universal ethic. It did not begin with the coming of Christ. Because Christian ethics is founded within the nature of God's character, and because every human being is made in the image of God, the ethical nature of God is inherent within everyone. All cultures recognize that murder, stealing, and lying are wrong.

- Christian ethics is a single, absolute standard for human behavior. It is applicable to everyone. This means that a unified standard exists in societies that practice Christian ethics.

- Christian morality is a high standard that is connected to the existence of sin. Because people cannot keep this standard perfectly, they feel guilty. That guilt may be overcome only by the recognition that Christ died for our sins and by trusting God to forgive. This recognition produces repentance and leads to a life of service and commitment to God.

- Christian ethics, being determined by God's character, has an ultimate foundation for law in society.

On the other hand, Humanist ethics comes from, and by, humans. Many implications are also derived from that fact.

- Humanist ethics is determined by individual and collective human experience, by reason, and by human intelligence.[1]

- Humanist ethics is pluralistic, that is, it has no single standard by which each person must determine his or her morality. This means that conflicting ethical standards may exist in societies that practice Humanist ethics.

- Humanist morality does not recognize the existence of sin because there is no standard of righteousness beyond humanity that may be violated.

- Humanist ethics, being determined by individual preferences, has no ultimate foundation for law in society. The basis

---

1 "It should be noted that secular Humanism is not so much a specific morality as it is a method for the explanation and discovery of rational moral principles." *A Secular Humanist Declaration,* 5.

for law is whatever the community thinks is right. Whatever prevailing community standard is most powerful becomes the ethical basis for judging individual human behavior under the law.

BRASS FACT Christian ethics is based upon the character of God. Humanist ethics is based upon human experience.

Ethical Requirements

Christian ethics requires full acceptance of divine authority as the basis for all human conduct. It allows no one the right to determine individual ethical standards. On the other hand, Humanist ethics rejects divine authority and allows each individual to accept or reject any portion of Christian ethics, or any other ethical system, as he or she may choose. Each individual is allowed to accept or reject any portion of an ethical system, as he or she may choose.

Christian ethics, being derived from divine authority, requires such character qualities as love, truth, and justice. Humanist ethics, being derived from personal human choice, cannot require those qualities.[2]

Because a Christian society recognizes that everyone sins, and because a Christian society looks to a single standard, it can call upon every sinner to repent. On the other hand, because a Humanist society does not recognize a single standard of righteousness, it cannot require anyone to change moral choices, except by force.

---

2 "A pluralistic, open democratic society allows all points of view to be heard. Any effort to impose an exclusive conception of Truth, Piety, Virtue, or Justice upon the whole of society is a violation of free inquiry. Clerical authorities should not be permitted to legislate their own personal views—whether moral, philosophical, political, educational, or social—for the rest of society." *A Secular Humanist Declaration*, 2.

Christian ethics requires forgiveness of one another because God through Christ has forgiven us. Humanist ethics cannot require forgiveness because every individual determines his or her own course of action.

BRASS FACT: Unlike Christian ethics, Humanist ethics cannot require love, truth, justice, forgiveness, or change in behavior.

Ethical Characteristics

Christian ethics is absolute, constant, fixed by God, and objective; Humanist ethics is relative,[1] situational, autonomous,[2] and subjective. Christian ethics emphasizes responsibilities because it is based on ethical values of love toward God and man; Humanist ethics emphasizes rights because it relates to selfish desires of individuals. Christian ethics finds freedom in divine authority; Humanist ethics seeks freedom from divine authority.[3] Christian ethics expects humanity to learn from God what is true and good; Humanist ethics expects everyone to make personal decisions to determine what is true and good. Christian ethics expects humanity to act according to God's standard of righteousness; Humanist ethics expects humanity to act according to personal or prevailing

---

1 "We are opposed to Absolutist morality, yet we maintain that objective standards emerge, and ethical values and principles may be discovered, in the course of ethical deliberation." *A Secular Humanist Declaration*, 4.
2 "We affirm that moral values derive their source from human experience. Ethics is *autonomous* and *situational*, needing no theological or ideological sanction. Ethics stems from human need and interest." *Humanist Manifesto II*, In Closing. (Emphasis in original.)
3 "The secular Humanist recognizes the central role of morality in human life . . . There is an influential philosophical tradition that maintains that ethics is an autonomous field of inquiry, that ethical judgments can be formulated independently of revealed religion, and that human beings can cultivate practical reason and wisdom and by its implication, achieve lives of virtue and excellence. . . . Thus secularists deny that morality needs to be deduced from religious belief or that those who do not espouse a religious doctrine are immoral." *A Secular Humanist Declaration*, 4.

ETHICS

social standards. Christian ethics constitutes a standard of divine "oughtness" by which everyone is judged by their fellow human beings and by God; Humanist ethics constitutes personal standards which, when carried to their logical conclusions, may allow tyrants and criminals to absolve themselves, in their own minds, from all wrong-doing. Christian ethics has an essential purpose to life—to glorify God and to serve fellow human beings. This purpose is grounded in the unchanging character of God. On the other hand, Humanist ethics has no essential purpose to life, since human life is thought to result from accidental evolutionary chance. This lack of purpose is grounded in the presumed evolutionary nature of mankind.

BRASS FACT: Christians find freedom in divine authority; Humanists seek freedom from divine authority.

ETHICS	Biblical Christianity	or	Secular Humanism
Foundation	Derived from God's character	or	Derived from human experience and reason
Standard	Single; unified	or	Plural; diversified
Moral behavior	Based on God's standards of righteousness	or	Based on standards that are acceptable to society
Law	Consistent as determined by God	or	Changes according to community opinion
Authority	Divine	or	Human
Characteristics	Absolute; emphasizes responsibility	or	Relative; emphasizes rights
Purpose	To glorify God and serve others	or	None—like evolution, it constantly changes.
Daily Living	Harmonious	or	Tense
SUMMARY	God	or	Man

Why Christian Ethics Is Superior

Harmonious Living

Christian ethics is inherently harmonious. Humanist ethics produces tensions between individuals and between individuals and their communities. When rightly followed, Christian ethics produces harmony in a society because of a single, authoritative standard. Humanist ethics, having the possibility of as many standards as there are individuals, is bound at times to produce social and political conflict. It is easy to see the contrast between the harmony of Christianity and the constant tensions of Humanism.

Since the Christian ethic is but a single standard, those who practice it must reject all other ethical standards. Only with a single standard can agreement exist regarding such ideals as the aim of morality, the nature of moral education, and the nature of justice. This agreement results ultimately in moral unity and stability in a society.

Since Humanist ethics is pluralistic, Humanists must be tolerant of all other ethical standards. Humanist ethics produces disagreements about the aim of morality, the nature of moral education, and the nature of justice. These disagreements result ultimately in moral permissiveness and instability in a society. Surely a harmonious society is better than one filled with conflicting ideological tensions.

Peace and harmony prevail when a society practices Christian ethics, but tensions and conflicts prevail when a society practices Humanist ethics.

Successful Foundation for Abiding Society

Christian ethics succeeds as a foundation for building an abiding society. Humanist ethics fails as a foundation for building a lasting society. A society based on Christian ethics is united and has agreed upon ethical foundations. It therefore has potential for success in building an abiding society. A society based on Humanist ethics is divided. It has not agreed upon ethical foundations; it is therefore likely to fail. Surely a lasting society is better than a failing society.

Responsible Behavior

Christian ethics requires personal responsibility toward others. Humanist ethics appeals to individual rights. Christian ethics, because it comes from God, operates from love toward God and one's fellow human beings, seeks the good of others. It requires truth, justice, kindness, forgiveness, and a host of other godly traits.[1] Christian ethics is unselfish.

Humanist ethics, because it comes from no authority beyond human beings, has no authority to persuade others to love; to tell the truth; or to be just, kind, and forgiving. Humanist ethics may be very selfish. Surely a society whose citizens assume responsibilities by loving one another is a better society than one whose individuals seek their own will.

Base to Establish Faith and Goodness

Christian ethics has grounds for establishing truth and goodness. Humanist ethics has no authoritative foundation for establishing truth or goodness. Humanists agree that for everyone to tell the truth is good. However, without God Humanists have no basis to establish principles that constitute truth and goodness. Because they have no universal ethical authority to which they may appeal, Humanists must rely on each individual's arbitrary definition of truth and goodness. Surely a society that has an authority for determining what constitutes truth and goodness is better than a society that has none.

---

1 Many biblical passages might be cited to demonstrate values of Christian ethics. Perhaps the most notable are the Ten Commandments (Exodus 20, Deuteronomy 5) and the Sermon on the Mount (Matthew 5–7).

Conclusion

Christian ethics was dominant in the Western World for many centuries, but Humanist ethics now appears to be more prevalent. The full consequences of following Humanist ethics are not yet evident. However, if present trends continue, disastrous results are sure to follow.

If there is no absolute beyond man's ideas, then there is no final appeal to judge between individuals and groups whose moral judgments conflict. We are merely left with conflicting opinions.

PLAYING WITH FIRE

Heather was bursting with a secret: "Gene, did you hear? Erin is in the news!"

Gene turned from the water cooler. "You're kidding! What happened?"

"She spilled a hot chocolate in her lap yesterday—boiling, just out of the microwave. Third degree burns. She's bringing a suit against Dinoes."

"Dinoes is a small restaurant. She won't get much out of them."

"That's what *you* think. Last week Dinoes quietly became a part of a national chain. She stands to get hundreds of thousands of dollars—maybe even two or three million."

Gene looked puzzled. "You mean, because she spilled hot chocolate in her lap at a restaurant?"

"Gene, the restaurant didn't have any warnings posted. And Dr. Wilton has warned Erin that her wound might become infected and cause major problems. She is going to miss work for a week or so."

"I don't understand, Heather. Everybody knows hot chocolate is supposed to be hot. Who would want it otherwise?"

"You're not playing fair, Gene. Erin is a human. She has her rights. That money-hungry company should have to pay up."

ETHICS

"I grew up on a farm," Gene reminisced. "One day I was helping a neighbor adjust the plows on his John Deere. He told me to hold a rod so he could insert it into a guide. My load was heavy and I lost my grip about the time he actuated the hydraulic pump. That's the reason I'm missing part of a fingernail now."

Gene pointed to his right index finger and continued. "I suppose I could have got a few thousand out of that."

"No! When you were a child, people didn't care about individuals, especially about farm workers. You were a Nobody. I'm thankful that now each person is a Somebody. Times have changed. Now individuals have their rights and they know them.

"Heather, I don't share your feelings. I believe when negligence is proved, the guilty person or business should be required to compensate for damages, but I do not believe extravagant and contrived lawsuits are beneficial to our society."

Heather spun on her heel. Gene heard her muttering something under her breath about "Neanderthal" and "chauvinist" as she scurried back to her office. And he was pretty sure he heard the words "a Nobody!" just before she slammed the door.

What kind of society embraces ethics which constantly emphasize individual rights relating to selfish desires?

Review Questions

1. From what is Christian ethics derived? From what is Humanist ethics derived?

2. Identify some foundational principles of Christian ethics, and then tell how they differ from foundational principles of Humanist ethics.

3. Identify some requirements of Christian ethics. How do they differ from their Humanist counterparts?

4. List some ways Christian ethics are superior to Humanist ethics?

5. Give examples of your interactions with those whose ethical values differ from yours.

Suggested Reading in Ethics

Davis, John Jefferson. *Evangelical Ethics: Issues Facing the Church Today*, Phillipsburg, NJ: Presbyterian and Reformed Publishing Co., 2004.

Geisler, Norman L. *Christian Ethics: Options and Issues*, Grand Rapids: Baker Book House, 1989.

Hightower, Terry M., Ed., *Biblical Ethics*, San Antonio: Shenendoah Church of Christ, 1991.

CHAPTER

BIOLOGY

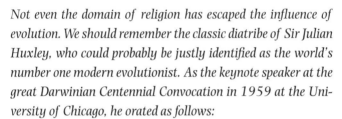

Not even the domain of religion has escaped the influence of evolution. We should remember the classic diatribe of Sir Julian Huxley, who could probably be justly identified as the world's number one modern evolutionist. As the keynote speaker at the great Darwinian Centennial Convocation in 1959 at the University of Chicago, he orated as follows:

> In the evolutionary system of thought there is no longer need or room for the supernatural. The earth was not created; it evolved. So did all the animals and plants that inhabit it, including our human selves, mind and soul, as well as brain and body. So did religion. Evolutionary man can no longer take refuge from his loneliness by creeping for shelter into the arms of a divinized father figure whom he himself has created.[1]

Biology is the study of life. The study of the origin of life is especially important both to Christians and Humanists. On this issue rests the very existence of both Christian and Humanist philosophies. For Christians, the doctrine of creation is foundational. For Humanists, the theory of evolution is the cornerstone doctrine on which hinges most other tenets of contemporary Humanism. Differences between Christian and Humanist worldviews in biology

---

1 Sir Julian Huxley, *Associated Press* dispatch, November 27, 1959.
  Remarks and quotation taken from Henry M. Morris, *The Troubled Waters of Evolution* (San Diego, CA: CLP publishers, 1974), 37.

are noted in seven categories, followed by arguments demonstrating why Christian biology is superior to Humanist biology.

 Whether life originated by creation or by evolution is the primary conflicting philosophical issue between Christians and Humanists.

Contrasting Biological Worldviews

Origin of life

There are basically only two points of view regarding the origin of life. One is the Christian belief that all life was created by God, according to the biblical record. This perspective contends that God designed all living things to reproduce after their own kinds (Genesis 1:1, 24–31; Psalm 8:3–4; John 1:3; Colossians 1:16; Ephesians 3:9; Hebrews 1:2, et al,). The other point of view is the Humanist belief that all life evolved by chance from a self-existing universe.[1] These viewpoints are mutually exclusive, although some try to compromise by styling themselves as "theistic" evolutionists. Theistic evolution not only contradicts biblical revelation but is also logically impossible. Within the evolutionary perspective are two separate categories. The most familiar is that of Charles Darwin (1809–1882), who proposed gradual evolutionary development in an upward progression through billions of years. Darwin's gradual evolutionary theory requires accidental chance, spontaneous generation, beneficial mutations, vast amounts of time, and missing links between species.

The most recent evolutionary hypothesis, proposed by Stephen Jay Gould (1941–2001), is called punctuated equilibrium. It holds that evolution developed by quantum leaps from one species to an-

---

1 "Science affirms that the human species is an emergence from natural evolutionary forces." *Humanist Manifesto II*, Second. "Religious Humanists regard the universe as self-existing and not created." *Humanist Manifesto I*, First.

other, rather than by gradual development. The punctuated equilibrium theory, put forward only because missing links cannot be found among fossils, still requires Darwinian mechanisms of spontaneous generation, natural selection, beneficial mutations, and accidental chance. However, the punctuated equilibrium theory is without any known scientific mechanism.

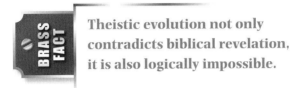

BRASS FACT Theistic evolution not only contradicts biblical revelation, it is also logically impossible.

Appeal to Science

Both Christians and Humanists appeal to science to support their contentions regarding the origin of life. Creationists think the evolutionary claim is not scientifically supportable.[2] On the other hand, evolutionists contend that because Christians appeal to a Creator—a supernatural being—the creationist belief cannot be based on findings of science. However, Christians believe their worldview is consistent not only with scientific facts, but also with scientific thought, that is, that the world is orderly and predictable. Creationists think the evolutionary worldview is illogical and inconsistent with science, because evolutionists believe in a world in which life forms are claimed to have developed accidentally by random chance.

Age of the Earth

Evolutionists claim that the universe is four to five billion years old, and that human beings originated about four million years ago. Such assumptions are essential for evolutionists, because they assume that given enough time, evolutionary development is possible. However, a very old universe has not been scientifically proven and is not scientifically verifiable. Creationists generally

---

2 For a devastating refutation of Darwin's evolutionary hypothesis, based on scientific evidences, consult Michael Behe, *Darwin's Black Box: The Biochemical Challenge to Evolution* (New York: The Free Press), 1996.

assume that the earth is comparatively young because a young earth seems more consistent not only with biblical revelation but also with scientific evidences.

Missing Links

For organic evolution to have occurred, one type of organism had to become another. If that occurred, evidence would surely be present in the fossil record, but the fossil record does not support the evolutionary contention of such links. For this reason, evolutionists have proposed the "punctuated equilibrium" theory of evolution, although it has no supporting mechanisms by which it may be understood to have operated. The fossil record indicates an explosion of different types of organisms at the lowest geological layers without ancestors. There is no evidence that organic evolution occurred. The evidence is that organisms were created. Creationists believe scientific evidence proves evolutionary claims are false, and that evidence of design in nature proves a designer.

Natural Selection

"Natural selection" is the designation given to the supposition that various forms of life have evolved with specific traits that better enable them to adapt to specific environmental pressures and thus to survive better than others of their kind. This idea has also been designated as "survival of the fittest." Natural selection has been considered a basic mechanism by which evolution progresses in an upward way. Natural selection does occur, but it cannot explain how one kind of organism can give rise to another kind of organism.

Spontaneous Generation

Spontaneous generation—life from non-life—is a cardinal doctrine of the theory of evolution. Although spontaneous generation is not scientifically verifiable, evolutionists must believe it because they reject supernaturalism. Creationists reject spontaneous generation because both natural and supernatural revelations argue against it.

BRASS FACT: Although spontaneous generation is not scientifically verifiable, evolutionists must believe it because they reject supernaturalism.

Mutations and Environmental Adaptations

Evolutionists propose, as part of natural selection, that mutations and environmental adaptations constitute a part of the mechanism for evolutionary development. However, no proven scientific verification exists for any information-increasing mutations. Without information-increasing mutations, there can be no upward progression of the evolutionary process.

BRASS FACT: Humanist biology provides no incentive beyond one's own will to strive for excellence.

BIOLOGY	Biblical Christianity	or	Secular Humanism
Origin of Life	Created	or	Evolved
Appeal to Science	Creation is consistent with scientific facts.	or	Evolution is inconsistent with scientific verifiability.
Age of Earth	Relatively young	or	Extremely old
Missing Links	No fossil evidence of organic evolution	or	Punctuated equilibrium
Spontaneous Generation	Life produces after its own kind.	or	Life came from non-life in a presumed pre-scientific age.
SUMMARY	God	or	Man

Why Christian Biology Is Superior

Better Explanation of Reproduction

Christian biology gives a better explanation for reproduction of life. Humanism requires that life evolve from one kind of organism to another; Christian biological thinking understands that life reproduces only after its own kind. Life has never been observed evolving from one genus to another (macro-evolution), but life is continually observed reproducing after its own kind (micro-evolution). In other words, a horse cannot evolve from an alligator, but collies and shepherds have evolved within the canine species.

Supportable By the Known Facts of Science

Creation, which requires design, is supported by scientific principles, such as the law of biogenesis, DNA, and the *second law of thermodynamics*. The absence of intermediate varieties of fossils argues against the theory of evolution and supports the creation perspective.

Better Explanation of Nature

Humanism requires an evolutionary worldview that operates on random chance; Christians believe in a created world that is orderly. While Humanist thinking about biology requires that humanity is only physical, Christian thinking about biology recognizes that humanity is both physical and spiritual.

Better Foundation for Living

Because Christians believe life has been created, they believe living things are subject to a Creator. Life has standards that determine behavior acceptable to the Creator, the all-powerful and all-knowing One who judges life. This understanding promotes better human behavior and makes for better communities. On the other hand, Humanists believe life originated by an evolutionary process and that it is subject to no power beyond mankind. All standards for conduct are imposed by self or others. People are not motivated to conduct themselves in any way beyond their own preferences. Humanist biology provides no incentive beyond one's own will to strive for excellence.

Conclusion

Humanist thinking regarding the evolutionary origin of life has frequently replaced the Christian worldview in the last century. The theory of evolution is the philosophical foundation for the professions of psychology and sociology. It has also impacted and sometimes significantly revamped other professions and aspects of life, such as religion, law, philosophy, ethics, medicine, history, education, entertainment, and the media. With the passing of time, scientific data are increasingly being marshaled against the theory of evolution. In thinking about these circumstances, Christians need not only to proclaim the falsity of the evolutionary theory, but also, and more important, to proclaim the truthfulness and significance of creation.

The most influential intellectuals in America and around the world are mostly naturalists, who assume that God exists only as an idea in the minds of religious believers. In our greatest universities, naturalism—the doctrine that nature is "all there is"—is the virtually unquestioned assumption that underlies not only natural science but intellectual work of all kinds . . . In the academic hierarchy, authority to describe "the way things really are" belongs to natural science, and the history of life belongs to evolutionary biology. This assignment of authority implies that the question of how living organisms came into existence is a matter of specialized knowledge, knowledge that is not available to persons outside the inner circle of science. Ordinary people thus have no alternative but to accept what the experts tell them about such matters, unless they want to be thought ignorant. If the consensus of opinion among evolutionary biologists is that biological evolution produced very complex living organisms by purposeless processes like mutations and selection, then that is the end of the matter. No one has authority to say otherwise.[1]

---

1 Phillip E. Johnson, *Reason in the Balance: The Case against Naturalism in Science, Law & Education* (Downers Grove, IL: InterVarsity Press, 1995), 7–8, 10–11.

CHRISTIANITY OR HUMANISM

PLAYING WITH FIRE

"Sean, since we are lifetime friends, I know I can ask you a question without being offensive." Sean and Ian were resting from a hard-fought game of handball. "How did you rationalize the Bible view of creation last month when you decided to become a Christian?"

"That's a fair question. You and I have held to the Big Bang belief since high school biology. I finally decided it took more faith to believe that than it did to believe God created the universe."

"How can you say that?" Ian was curious. "Creation is myth."

"Before I became a Christian, I believed the 'it was a miracle' bit was a copout. I always enjoyed challenging Christians to replicate creation in a laboratory."

"A particular miracle, even according to the Christian thinking, occurs only once, so it cannot be scientifically verified. I don't see how a rational man like you came to accept a fairy tale religion."

"Ian, have you really thought about the Big Bang? Scientists say it occurred only once and it cannot be proved in a laboratory. I've never heard of anyone who believes otherwise."

"You're right about that, of course, but my view is philosophical. A wise old man told me one time: 'No, we cannot prove the Big Bang, and we probably never will. But that belief is far better than the alternative.' I think he was right."

"In other words, your belief of how things came into existence is based on nothing more than somebody's supposition. It's sort of like a miracle except in the case of the Big Bang nobody claims that witnesses have attested to it."

Ian pondered that thought for a few seconds. "I never thought of it like that, but I guess you're right. But for me to accept your belief would completely mess up my politics, my entertainment, my—well, it would turn my life upside down. And I'm pretty comfortable right now."

Does life comes from life or does life comes from nonlife? Does intelligence come from intelligence or does intelligence come from lifeless chemicals? Prove your answers.

BIOLOGY

Review Questions

1. Name and describe two different evolutionary theories.
2. How do Christians and Humanists differ in their appeal to, and use of science regarding the origin of life?
3. How do Christians and Humanists differ in their evaluation of the earth's time span? In your opinion, how does one's belief about the age of the earth affect one's understanding of the origin of life?
4. How does the fossil record support creation? How does it nullify the gradual theory of evolution? How do evolutionists seek to overcome missing links in the fossil record?
5. Identify several mechanisms in the gradual theory of evolution, and show how Christians may refute them.
6. What is meant by the following terms? Natural selection, spontaneous generation, information-increasing mutations, and environmental adaptations.
7. What scientific principles may be used to support creation?
8. How may Christian thinking about the origin of life be considered superior to Humanist thinking about the origin of life?
9. How is an understanding of differing perspectives regarding the origin of life meaningful to you?

Suggested Readings in Biology

Behe, Michael. *Darwin's Black Box: The Biochemical Challenge to Evolution*, New York: The Free Press, 1996.

Johnson, Phillip. *Darwin on Trial*, Downers Grove, IL: InterVarsity Press, 1991.

CHAPTER

MEDICINE

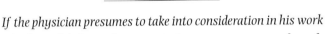

If the physician presumes to take into consideration in his work whether a life has value or not, the consequences are boundless and the physician becomes the most dangerous man in the state.[1]

—Dr. Christoph Hufeland (1762–1836)

Although medicine is an ancient and honorable profession, it has undergone tremendous technological advancement in the last century. Marvelous benefits have been received from medical practitioners, for which all may be thankful. Even so, both Christians and Humanists are concerned about the philosophical underpinnings of medicine. Everyone knows that whatever the prevailing governing philosophical principles of medicine may be, they have practical ramifications in many areas of medical practice. These relate to issues in health, human life, reproduction, society, and science. In America, since the mid-twentieth century, the field of medicine has become a battleground for the competing ideologies of Christianity and Humanism.

---

1 Wertham, Fredric, *The German Euthanasia Program: Excerpts from a Sign for Cain: An Explanation of Human Violence* (Cincinnati, OH: Hayes Publishing Company, Inc., 1980), 25.

CHRISTIANITY OR HUMANISM

BRASS FACT: Our society's conflicting medical practices will be settled according to which medical philosophy—Christian or Humanist—wins over the other.

Contrasting Medical Worldviews

Philosophical Foundations of Medicine

Philosophically, the Christian perspective regarding medicine is founded upon belief in God, that is, upon supernaturalism. Christian medical practice endorses the "sanctity of life" philosophy. It contends that every human being is made in the image of God. Medical treatment must therefore be impartial, as it is based upon the inherent worth of all individuals. It is pro-life! Moreover, since only human beings are made in God's image, people are to be treated better than animals.

Humanist philosophy regarding medicine is based on naturalism, materialism, and scientism. Humanist medicine endorses the so-called, but misnamed, "quality of life" philosophy. It is what Humanists call "pro-choice"! Medical treatment is therefore selective and based upon desirability and productivity of individuals. It ultimately considers people to be "naked apes," and therefore may be treated no better than other animals.

BRASS FACT: The pro-choice philosophy contends that an individual has worth only if desired or productive.

Issues Related to Good Medical Health

Since Christians believe human beings are both physical and spiritual in nature, then good health requires that both body and spirit function properly. Therefore, Christians believe medicine

MEDICINE

should treat the physical, while recognizing its interaction with the spiritual.

Humanists think human beings are only physical, that medicine relates solely to the physical body. They generally reject the idea that the physical body can be affected by an individual's spiritual condition, or that by treating a spiritual malady the physical body can be improved.

Human Life Issues in Medicine

Differing concepts regarding the origin of life are at the root of conflict between Christian and Humanist worldviews regarding human life issues in medicine. Since Christians believe that God created humans in His own image, that human life begins at conception, and that God prohibits murder, they also believe abortion, infanticide, euthanasia, and suicide are morally wrong, and should not be medically acceptable.

Since Humanists do not believe humans resulted from divine creativity, they believe human communities may declare whatever they choose regarding the origin and disposition of human life. Human reasoning, apart from divine sanctions, allows that personhood be declared to begin only at birth, or even after birth, so abortion, infanticide, euthanasia, and suicide may not only be medically permitted but also declared as matters of individual human rights.

Humanists believe that abortion, infanticide, euthanasia, and suicide are matters of individual civil rights.

Reproductive Issues Related to Medicine

Since Christians believe mankind came from God, then Christians believe people should confine their reproductive activities to those God has decreed. Surrogate motherhood, cloning, and similar issues should not be legalized, as these practices violate biblical ethics.

Since Humanists believe mankind evolved, then people may direct their own evolutionary paths as they think desirable. That means surrogate motherhood, genetic engineering, and cloning are but a few of the many legitimate ways people may engage in reproductive activities.

Some Social Issues Related to Medicine

In Christian communities, medicine generally operates through free enterprise. Medicine is pro-family. (Parental approval is required for medications and procedures involving minors.) Christians generally believe mind-altering drugs should not be legalized unless medically prescribed.

In Humanist communities, medicine generally operates through socialism. Medicine becomes anti-family as parental approval is not always required for medications and procedures involving minors. Humanists generally believe some mind-altering drugs—marijuana, for example—should be legalized.

For Humanists, medical research should never be restricted by ethical considerations.

Scientific Issues Related to Medicine

Christians claim Scripture as the sole basis for determining medical ethics and practices. Medical research and practice should be confined to biblical ethics. Medicine is a tool of healing to all, regardless of wealth or power. It blesses humanity.

Humanists claim science as the basis for determining ethical practices such as those related to sexual orientation, incest, and such like; therefore, medical research should never be restricted by ethical considerations. Medicine then becomes, potentially, a tool of death via abortion, infanticide, and euthanasia, especially to the poor, weak, and undesirable. It can curse humanity.

History Demonstrates Differing Results from Differing Medical Worldviews

The Judeo-Christian belief in the sanctity of human life has throughout many centuries given great motivation to unselfish and sacrificial medical practices around the world. It devotes itself to prolonging human life. It spawns medical care for the sick and the poor. It produces medical care for the orphan and the widow. History verifies this is the worldview that initiated the building of hospitals. Beneficial results from medical practices coming from the Christian worldview are so extensive and so generally known that there is no need to demonstrate them by pointing to particular historical situations.

On the other hand, the destructive medical results of the Humanist worldview may be illustrated from happenings in Germany in the first half of the twentieth century. The Darwinian belief that man is but a product of evolutionary development affected the German medical profession. In the decade of the 1920s, a small book was circulated among medical practitioners, especially psychiatrists and psychologists. This book, *The Release of the Destruction of Life Devoid of Value*, contented that some human lives were without value. The medical profession appointed itself the task of destroying those lives by the best method possible—the gas chamber. Before Hitler came to power, 275,000 German men, women, and children, whose lives were "devoid of value," died in gas chambers. Hitler merely continued the horrid method already initiated by the German medical profession.

If lives may be considered devoid of value because of poor physical or mental health, why cannot they also be considered devoid of value for other reasons—such as belonging to what may be considered an "inferior race"? When applied to medicine, Humanist philosophies will eventually become destructive to every human life that the rich and powerful consider devoid of value.

CHRISTIANITY OR HUMANISM

While it is true that atrocities have been instigated by those professing a Christian worldview—the Crusades (A.D. 1096–1270); the Spanish Inquisition (A.D. 1350–1400)—those actions were totally inconsistent with the nature of genuine Christianity. However, the deaths in Germany's gas chambers were consistent with the philosophy of Humanism.

MEDICINE	Biblical Christianity	or	Secular Humanism
Foundation	Sanctity of Life	or	Economic "quality" of Life
Treatments	Recognizes both physical and spiritual nature	or	Recognizes only physical nature
Human Life	Prohibits human right to choose death	or	Sanctions human right to choose death
Reproduction	Only within God's marital decree	or	Personal choice regarding sexual permissiveness
Drugs	Mind-altering, addictive drugs should be illegal.	or	Mind-altering, addictive drugs should be legalized.
Distribution	Scripture-based	or	Man-determined
Regulation	Operates through free enterprise; is pro-family	or	Operates through civil and social authority; may be anti-family
SUMMARY	God	or	Man

Why Christian Medicine Is Superior

Christians Have Greater Respect for Human Life

Christian medical practice considers the whole of individuals because it treats both the physical and spiritual nature. It understands that human life is sacred, and therefore prohibits medical practices associated with abortion, euthanasia, infanticide, and assisted suicide. Christian medical practice recognizes equality in the worth of individuals, and therefore must be applied impartially. Christians reject the concept that medicine may be used as a destructive tool to manipulate social values according to wishes of the rich, powerful, or elite.

MEDICINE

Absolute Moral Standards Produce Better Societies

The moral standards of Christian medical practice are based upon biblical ethical principles. Christian medical practice sanctions marriage, and therefore rejects the promiscuous sexual practices of unmarried persons. It considers the sanctity of human life, and therefore condemns medical practices related to human cloning, surrogate motherhood, cryonics, and the like. Because Christians recognize that biblical authority is given to the family to care for its own, Christian medicine looks to the family rather than to the State for decisions related to technically prolonging the life of a family member. Christian medical practice operates best within free enterprise, rather than in a system of socialism.

Christian medical practice is better because it contributes to holding families together, produces greater moral purity within society, and gives families greater responsibility and authority to care for their own. The medical system is best that does these things.

Conclusion

Medicine has historically been associated with religion. The nature of a society's medical practice is closely associated with that society's religion. When evidence abounds that medical practices within a society are undergoing drastic changes, that evidence will also indicate that the general religious attitudes of that society are changing. The field of medicine is a battleground wherein the Christian and Humanist worldviews are currently contending against each other. Our society's medical practices will be settled according to which of these two philosophies wins.

While the Humanist approach to biomedical ethics is to play God, the Christian approach is to use medical advances to serve God. Humanists believe that man is sovereign over life; Christians hold that God is sovereign over it.[1]

---

1 Norman L. Geisler, *Christian Ethics: Options and Issues* (Grand Rapids, MI: Baker Book House, 1994), 179.

CHRISTIANITY OR HUMANISM

PLAYING WITH FIRE

Rudi and Hilda were concerned about their little Katrin. Since birth she had had respiratory problems. She often awoke in the night, struggling for breath. Their family physician, a long-time friend, was doing all he could, but the problem was not improving.

"She needs the attention of a specialist," he told them, "and I can send her to one. But you need to know that once Katrin's condition is known by the State, her medical records will be sent to the Reich Health Ministry for review. If the panel of three physicians unanimously agrees that her condition is a burden to society, a euthanasia warrant will be issued and Katrin will be transferred to a Children's Specialty Department."

Dr. Mueller tried to continue, then hesitated and stopped.

"That is good," Rudi replied excitedly. "At the Children's Specialty Department, she can get the treatment she needs."

"I'm afraid you missed the word *euthanasia*." Dr. Mueller's voice was breaking; Rudi did not interrupt. "Euthanasia means 'good death.' According to a law passed a few months ago, October 1939, the Fuehrer has authority to eliminate a 'life unworthy of life'—the elderly and chronically ill—and even those of the wrong race. I have no doubt that Katrin would be pronounced unfit. I am sorry to—"

Terror gripped the faces of Rudi and Hilda as the doctor's voice faded. "You mean they would kill her?" Rudi could hardly control himself. "They can't do that. She's our baby. You are our doctor. You could stop them."

Dr. Mueller gently placed his hand on Rudi's shoulder and took Hilda's trembling hand: "If I refer her to a specialist, I will have no control over how she's treated. It's the law."

When a culture rejects belief in a Higher Power, whose laws determine how citizens are treated? How can the State be forbidden to take human life at will?

Review Questions

1. Describe differences in philosophical foundations of Christian medicine and Humanist medicine.

2. How do human-life issues in Christian medicine differ from those in Humanist medicine?

3. How do reproductive issues differ?

4. How do social issues differ?

5. How do scientific issues differ?

6. How do the results of medicine practiced from a Christian perspective differ from those practiced from a Humanist perspective?

7. In what ways may Christian medical practices be said to be superior to Humanist medical practices?

8. How do you imagine medical practices would differ from what they now are if they were practiced altogether from a Humanist perspective?

Suggested Readings in Medicine

Grant, George. Grand *Illusions: The Legacy of Planned Parenthood,* Brentwood, TN: Wolgemuth & Hyatt, Publishers, Inc. 1988.

Wertham, Fredric. The German Euthanasia Program: Excerpts from "A Sign for Cain," Cincinnati, OH: Hayes Publishing Co., Inc. 1980.

CHAPTER

PSYCHOLOGY

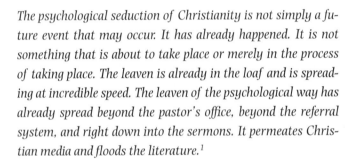

The psychological seduction of Christianity is not simply a future event that may occur. It has already happened. It is not something that is about to take place or merely in the process of taking place. The leaven is already in the loaf and is spreading at incredible speed. The leaven of the psychological way has already spread beyond the pastor's office, beyond the referral system, and right down into the sermons. It permeates Christian media and floods the literature.[1]

As a process, psychology is the study of the human mind as determined by human behavior. Psychology as a profession became significant only after Charles Darwin proposed a mechanism for the theory of evolution (1859). Contemporary psychological concepts originated out of a naturalistic and evolutionary worldview. Wilhelm Wundt founded the first psychological laboratory in 1879.

Sigmund Freud (1856–1939), an Austrian physician, was the first major influential psychologist. He theorized that unconscious motives control much of human behavior. After considerable influence in psychiatry and psychology, Freud's influence waned only to be followed by the behavioral psychology initiated by

---

1 Martin and Deidre Bobgan, *Psychoheresy: The Psychological Seduction of Christianity* (Santa Barbara, CA: EastGate Publishers, 1987), 7.

John B. Watson (1878–1958) and popularized primarily by B. F. Skinner (1904–1990). Contemporary Humanist psychology follows neither the psychoanalytic approach of Freud nor the behavioral approach of Skinner. Humanists now generally shun behaviorism because it denies individual freedom and free will.

Current Humanist psychology is a "third force" that attempts to avoid the dilemma of studying a free mind made up of only synapses responding to stimuli. An understanding of the modern profession of psychology is aided by observing differences in Christian and Humanist psychological values. After these different values are presented, arguments will be given to demonstrate the superiority of Christian psychological values over Humanist psychological values.

Professional psychology was popularized by the theory of evolution. Psychoanalysis first dominated it, then behaviorism, and now Humanism.

Contrasting Psychological Worldviews

Philosophical Foundations and Presuppositions

For Christians, psychology is philosophically based on an understanding of humanity as presented in Scripture, namely, that people have a *psyche*, that is, a soul; Humanist rejects the concept of the soul. Unlike Christian beliefs about psychology, Humanist beliefs about psychology presuppose that humanity originated solely from a physical background, rather than from having been made in the image of God. Humanists do not recognize that individuals have a spiritual nature or that they are destined for eternal existence after death. While Christians understand human nature through both divine revelation and human research, Humanists deny the relevancy of divine revelation. Christians therefore contend that Humanists, starting with false and inadequate premises about psychology, cannot avoid arriving at false conclusions.

Psychological Perspectives

Christians hold that the brain (matter) and the mind (spirit) are two different things. Christians may therefore be said to be dualistic. On the other hand, Humanists hold that the brain and the mind are one and the same thing. Humanist psychology may therefore be said to be monistic. Christians recognize that God is real, that humanity was created in God's image, that people have both a physical and a spiritual nature, that everyone sins, that human existence is for both time and eternity, and that everyone is answerable to God. On the other hand, Humanists consider God to be but a mythical figure, that humanity evolved, that a person has only a physical nature, that everyone is basically good, that human existence is only temporal since there is no eternity for individuals, and that people are answerable only to mankind. Christians understand that human memory continues, although physical brain cells can change. For Christians, this indicates that the mind is more than just matter. On the other hand, Humanists, because they consider the brain and the mind one and the same thing, have no explanation for memory and other mental functions. Christians understand that consciousness is a supernatural phenomenon that continues after death; Humanists generally deny the existence of such an immortal consciousness because it implies a creator.

All Christian and most Humanist psychologists accept the view that people have free will. Because Christian psychology is dualistic, it is consistent with free will and the nature and credibility of ideas. Humanist psychology is monistic and inconsistent because it holds that the existence of free will and the nature and credibility of ideas are accidents of chance.

Contemporary psychology has distorted humanity's understanding of itself by denying that people are made in the image of God.

CHRISTIANITY OR HUMANISM

Human Nature and Human Values

Christians understand human traits are received from God because mankind was made in the image of God; Humanists believe human potential is derived from nature. Christians believe people should rely on God, should be Christ-centered, and should deny self; Humanists believe people should rely on self and personal feelings, and become self-actualized. Christians understand that many mental illnesses are caused by sin, and that greater mental health is possible by a person's becoming right with God. On the other hand, Humanists often think that many mental illnesses come from believing in God, and that greater mental health is often possible by achieving full human potential.

Attitudes toward Suffering

Christians believe suffering can enable an individual to achieve a better life. Humanists find no meaning in suffering and seek to alleviate it altogether.

Christians and Humanists differ in their understandings of guilt. Christians believe individual feelings of guilt result from sin and are genuine. To obtain freedom from guilt, an individual needs to repent and seek the forgiveness found in Christ. Humanists believe individual feelings of guilt are psychological only, inasmuch as evil is thought to come, not from individuals but from environment and society. To obtain freedom from guilt, an individual should continue participating in those activities that cause guilt, and soon the guilt will dissipate.

 Humanist psychology operates on the premise that people are not sinners. Humanists contend that people are basically good.

Evil Related to Individuals and Societies

The existence of evil in society is considered by Christians to be because people are sinners. Christians believe individual sins cause cultural and social evils, that when individuals do right, society is benefited. For Humanists, the existence of evil in society is considered to have originated in cultural and social institutions. Humanists believe evil generally does not originate with individuals, because people are thought to be basically good. For Humanists, when society rids itself of evil, individuals can "learn" to do right.

The Spiritual Nature of Humanity

In the New Testament, the spiritual nature of man is characterized as being either of the old man of sin or of the new man in Christ. The old man of sin is characterized as follows:

- Carnally minded (John 3:6; Romans 8:5–8; 1 Corinthians 3:3; 15:48).
- Alienated from God (Ephesians 2:12; James 4:4).
- Fleshly (Colossians 2:18), self-willed (2 Peter 2:10).
- Producing iniquity and death (Romans 1:21–32; 6:21; 8:6; 1 Corinthians 6:9–10; Ephesians 2:3, 5; Titus 3:3; 1 Peter 4:3; 1 John 5:19).

The new man in Christ is characterized as follows:

- Spiritually minded (Romans 8:9–14; 1 Corinthians 3:16; 6:19; Galatians 4:6).
- Becoming like Christ (Ephesians 4:22; Colossians 3:5).
- Powerful (2 Timothy 1:7).
- Strengthened (Ephesians 3:16; Colossians 1:11).
- Victorious (Romans 8:37; 1 Corinthians 15:57; 2 Corinthians 2:14; 1 John 4:4; 5:4; Revelation 12:11) in giving and serving (Romans 12:1, 8; Matthew 20:26–28; John 13:14–15).

- Both man and God (Romans 7:6; 12:11; 14:18; Galatians 5:13; Ephesians 6:5–8; Philippians 2:17; Hebrews 9:14; 12:28).

Because Humanists do not recognize the existence of sin, they cannot comprehend human behavior related to redemption, repentance, or turning to God.

Old Man of Sin	or	New Man in Christ
Carnally Minded	or	Spiritually Minded
Alienated from God	or	Victorious
Self-willed	or	Giving and serving
Producing iniquity and death	or	Promoting harmony, life, and service

Why Christian Psychology Is Superior

Consistent Psychological Views

Christian psychological views are consistent with their philosophical foundations, but Humanist psychological perspectives are not consistent with theirs. Since Christian psychological views are philosophically based on both natural and supernatural revelation, the conclusions regarding human behavior, related to both the physical and spiritual aspects of human nature, may be consistently applied. Were Humanist psychological views applied consistently to its philosophical base of naturalism—that is, the theory of evolution—it would have no consistent explanations for human behavior because human behavior would be derived from random chance.

Better Explanations of Human Behavior

Christian psychological perspectives give better explanations of human nature and behavior. Because Christian psychology, derived from an understanding that humanity is both physical and spiritual, better recognizes the nature of humanity, it can give better answers to human problems related to sin and its consequences. It better understands the problem of guilt and freedom from guilt.

It can call for repentance—turning toward God. It can give assurances of redemption.

BRASS FACT Unlike Humanists, Christians have a definitive, absolute, and positive ethical standard by which to evaluate human behavior.

PSYCHOLOGY	Biblical Christianity	or	Secular Humanism
Foundation	Physical and spiritual natures; (Psyche, the soul)	or	Physical only
Perspective	Brain (matter) and mind (spirit) are separate; life after death	or	Brain and mind are one and the same; no afterlife
Human Nature	Made in God's image; humanity is endowed with traits from God.	or	Derived from the natural world; humanity has worldly potential.
Mental Health	Is possible by being right with God	or	Is possible by achieving full potential
Suffering	Seeks lessons from suffering to produce a better life	or	Seeks to eliminate suffering; it is of no benefit.
Guilt	Caused by sin; cured by repentance	or	Caused by environment; cured by continuing the guilt-causing activity
Evil	Caused by individual sin; cure is to think and do right.	or	Caused by social sin; cure is to improve social environments.
SUMMARY	God	or	Man

Conclusion

Humanist psychology has had an uncertain sound, changing from Freudian to behavioral to a third force. Currently, Humanist psychology is in a state of chaos, having no solid foundation. Even so, Humanist psychology is extremely influential in major professions like education, sociology, medicine, and law, as well as upon people individually. People once generally consulted the Bible for guidance to life. Now, more and more often, they look for guidance from psychologists who have no appreciation for biblical values and no certain standard of values. Humanist psychology has conditioned humanity to look within for the power of positive thinking rather than to trust God. Humanist psychology has changed people's perception of reality from objective knowledge to that of subjective experiences. It has changed the perception of reality from that of *being* to that of *becoming.* Humanist psychology has thereby contributed to changing considerations of Christianity from being historically fixed to being progressively changing. Moreover, contemporary psychology has distorted humanity's understanding of itself by denying that people are made in the image of God. If society began to act with conviction that humanity is made in the image of God, the building blocks of Humanist psychology would come tumbling down.

It is difficult to document such a thing as the general attitude of a profession. But the hostility of most psychologists to Christianity is very real . . . It is a curious hostility, for most psychologists are not aware of it. Their lack of awareness is due mostly to sheer ignorance of what Christianity is—for that matter, or what any religion is. The universities are so secularized that most academics can no longer articulate why they are opposed to Christianity. They merely assume that for all rational people the question of being a Christian was settled—negatively—at some time in the past.[1]

---

1 Paul C. Vitz, *Psychology as Religion: The Cult of Self-Worship*, (Grand Rapids: William B. Eerdmans Publishing Co., 1977), 12

PSYCHOLOGY

PLAYING WITH FIRE

Dorothy Caso gazed at the sheet-draped body of a young women being wheeled in the ambulance and sobbed into the Channel 9 news camera: "The mental health system failed my son. He has always needed help. If someone had listened to me, that young mother would still be alive."

Sonny Caso was a violent child who became a substance abuser in his teens. Then at 21, he walked into a local convenience store, pulled his gun, and shot a twenty-three-year-old mother of three in cold blood. A week earlier, he had been pronounced cured and was dismissed from the state mental health center.

Although the psychiatrist in charge of Sonny's case could not divulge much information, he did make this comment: "Funding is needed for more preventive mental health programs, along with medication and treatment for addicts."

Sonny Caso is now serving a life sentence for murder. His mother blames the mental health system, his psychiatrist blames a lack of funding, and three children go to sleep every night without their mother's kisses. They are not old enough to blame anyone.

What trait of Humanism is evident regarding the existence of evil in society?

Review Questions

1. Define psychology. Give a brief review of its historical development as a profession.

2. What are some foundational differences between Christian and Humanist psychological perspectives?

3. Define the psychological perspectives of *dualism* and *monism*.

4. Describe how Christians and Humanists differ psychologically regarding human values.

5. What is the Christian attitude toward suffering?
6. What is the Humanist attitude toward suffering?
7. How do Christians and Humanists differ psychologically regarding guilt?
8. How do Christians and Humanists differ psychologically regarding the existence of evil in individuals and society?
9. How may Christian view of psychology be said to be superior to Humanist view of psychology?
10. What dangers await Christians who go to Humanist psychologists for counseling?

Suggested Reading in Psychology

Vitz, Paul. *Psychology as Religion: The Cult of Self-Worship*, Grand Rapids: Wm. B. Eerdmans Publishing Company. 1977.

CHAPTER

8

SOCIOLOGY

> *The matriarchal welfare state, even when pursuing "pro-family" goals, has produced family-disruptive results. The assorted crises that mark the history of our domestic policy debates—the poverty crisis, the ageism crisis, the teen pregnancy crisis, the overpopulation crisis, the juvenile delinquency crisis—have all become, intentionally or unintentionally, vehicles to expand the power of the State at the expense of the autonomy of its old adversary, the family.*[1]

Sociology is the study of the history, development, organization, values, and problems of people living together as social groups and in various social institutions: the family, the church, and the state. As a profession, sociology is comparatively recent in world history, having originated with the Frenchman Auguste Comte (1798–1857). It came out of "Enlightenment" thinking. While the Bible does not discuss sociology as a profession or as a discipline of study, it does discuss social relationships and institutions—family, church, and civil government. Whatever a community's prevailing social values may be—Christian or Humanist—they influence that society's public policies. Sociology is therefore closely associated with law and politics. Christian and Humanist world-

---

1 Allan C. Carlson, *Family Questions: Reflections on the American Social Crisis* (New Brunswick: Transaction Books, 1990), 273.

views regarding sociology are contrasted, after which arguments are given to show why Christian ideas about society are superior to Humanist ideas about society. By implication, these arguments also demonstrate why Christian thinking about law and politics is superior to Humanist thinking about law and politics.

As a profession, sociology originated out of so-called "Enlightenment" thinking to influence public policies through law and politics.

Contrasting Sociological Worldviews

Foundations of Society

For Christians, society looks to God's word for regulation of the individual, family, church, and nation. Each social order is considered to have its separate roles and responsibilities—although these may sometimes overlap. For Humanists, society looks to the State for regulation of all human life and institutions. Humanists want sociology to be designated as a science—it does not function according to recognized scientific procedures—in order to give their sociological studies greater credibility to produce change in social orders that conform to their ideological presuppositions. By relying on law and politics to enforce their sociological values, Humanists derive greater meaning from their sociological work. Because Christians in America have lived where social, legal, and political authority were previously thought to come from God, many Christians have not been active in legal and political efforts to sustain their sociological values. Many Christians therefore have been caught off guard in their discovery that Humanists use legal and political arenas to change social conditions.

Regarding mankind, Christians believe God is active in human affairs, individuals have freedom of choice (free will) to do either good or bad, and individuals may be alienated from God as a result of bad personal choices. On the other hand, Humanists believe there is no God, individuals are basically good, and people are not guilty of doing evil. In essence, the conflict between Christians and Humanists in sociology is between Christian belief in individual free will and freedom, and Humanist philosophy that people think and act according to social conditioning.

- *Civil government:* Christian belief is that civil government is under God, limited in authority to the administration of justice, and co-equal, under God, in authority with family and church government. Humanists believe there is no God, so civil governments have unlimited authority to regulate whatever they will over all institutions.

   Humanists, via civil government, seek to regulate education and economics in order to mold and control society.

- *Education:* Christians recognize the family and the church as the best agencies for teaching Christian social values. Humanists seek to utilize government schools to teach Humanist social values.

- *Economics:* Capitalism seems most favorable to Christians since it permits the building of a free society where the family is financially responsible to provide for its own, and where voluntary assistance is granted to the needy. Socialism seems most favorable to Humanists, since it enables them to build what they might call a self-actualized society where the State redistributes citizens' wealth, ideally providing a guaranteed minimum annual wage for everyone.

 Socialism grants Humanists greater ease in molding society through education and economics.

Social Values

Christians require that marriage be monogamous—one man with one woman for a lifetime. Humanists permit marital alternatives: monogamous, polygamous, communal, serial, heterosexual, and homosexual. Christian sexual conduct is restricted to what is morally permitted by God; sexual conduct under Humanism is generally permissive. Christians require that not only the authority but also the roles and responsibilities of men and women be different; Humanism requires that these be equalitarian. Christians define the family as a husband and his wife, possibly with their children; Humanism defines the family as two or more adults, possibly with their children. (The Humanist definition of the family allows for legalized marital unions of the same sex.)

For Christians, family authority is subservient primarily to God, and, secondarily to the State; for Humanists, family authority is independent of God and is altogether subservient to the State.

For Christians, the church is primarily responsible for proclaiming the message of the gospel, but it is also free to teach truths of God regarding all social aspects of life. For Humanists, the message of the gospel is denied, even though Humanists seek to use the agency of the church to teach Humanist beliefs. While the primary means for teaching Christian social values is the family and the church, the primary means for teaching Humanist social values is government schools. Humanists seek to annul all Christian influence—sociological, legal, political, economic—in public policy by claiming the necessity of a constitutional "separation of church and state."

Source of Evil

Christians accept biblical teaching that everyone sins (Romans 3:10, 23). It places responsibility for evil in society upon individuals. (See James 2:13–16.) Humanists operate on the assumption that everyone is basically good. They claim that evil comes from societies, not from individuals.

Unlike Humanists, Christians believe that a better society results from better individuals.

Methods for Changing Society

Because Christians recognize sin in everyone, they seek to improve society through motivating everyone to become better by conforming to biblical standards. A better society results from better individuals.

Humanists believe Christian social standards are invalid because they are based on the character of God—a God that Humanists think does not exist. They seek to produce revolutionary social changes through legal and political procedures that include changing Christian beliefs and conduct about sex, marriage, and family.

SOCIOLOGY	Biblical Christianity	or	Secular Humanism
Foundation	God's word	or	The State
Perspective	Sustained by obedience to God	or	Sustained by legal and political policies
Values	Individuals believe and act according to God's word.	or	Individuals believe and act according to social conditioning.
Civil Government	Under God—co-equal with family and church governments	or	Without God—over family and church governments
Education	Family and church produce godly values.	or	State produces contemporary social values.
Economics	Capitalism—promotes industry, responsibility and benevolence	or	Socialism—promotes redistribution of wealth by State
Marriage	Restricted to monogamy of male and female	or	Permissive; anything goes.
Family	Consists of husband, wife, and their children.	or	Consists of two or more adults and possibly children
Church	Desires Christian influence in all areas of life	or	Desires separation of Christian influence within society
SUMMARY	God	or	Man

CHRISTIANITY OR HUMANISM

Why Christian Sociology Is Superior

A Stable Society

Christian social values produce a stable society. A society with the family as its basic unit, as in Christianity, is a stable society. A society with the individual as its basic unit, as in Humanism, is an unstable one. Humanism is anti-family. The declarations of Humanists are not worded so as to portray an anti-family bias, yet that is their logical and ultimate consequence. Humanism stresses individual rights, individual autonomy, and human equality.

Typical Humanist declarations when viewed from the perspective of individual rights seem positive, yet when viewed from the perspective of the family are really negative. Humanists believe "the right to birth control, abortion, and divorce should be recognized."[1] They claim that "short of harming others or compelling them to do likewise, individuals should be permitted to express their sexual proclivities and pursue their life-styles as they desire."[2] They believe "the individual must experience a full range of *civil liberties* in all societies." This "includes a recognition of an individual's right to die with dignity, euthanasia, and the right to suicide."[3]

Humanists "believe in maximum individual autonomy consonant with social responsibility . . . the possibilities of individual freedom of choice exist in human life and should be increased."[4]

Christian social values produce a more stable society than do Humanist social values.

Humanist emphasis on individual autonomy and rights, rather than on responsibilities, plays havoc with the family. Obedience, duty, fidelity, humility, commitment, and loyalty are not empha-

---

1 *Humanist Manifesto II*, Sixth.
2 *Humanist Manifesto II*, Sixth.
3 *Humanist Manifesto II*, Seventh.
4 *Humanist Manifesto II*, Fifth.

sized in a Humanist culture. "With monotonous regularity, the selfist literature sides with those values that encourage divorce, breaking up, dissolution of marital or family ties."[5] When the family is unstable, society becomes unstable. Society is then subject to decay and destruction. A stable and abiding society is surely better than an unstable and deteriorating society.

Fixed Standards

Christian social values operate on fixed standards. While Christians operate on absolute standards fixed by God, Humanists operate on flexible, indefinite, and relative standards. This means that Christian sociological norms are constant, and individuals may recognize their success or failure in conforming to absolute standards.

Since Humanist sociological standards are constantly changing, individuals can never be sure whether or not they are conforming to socially acceptable standards. For individuals to feel secure in conforming to acceptable standards is surely better than for them to feel insecure.

Individual Social Responsibilities

Christian social values emphasize individual social responsibilities rather than personal rights. Christians emphasize responsibility to others, but Humanism requires no responsibility other than to abide by prevailing legal ordinances. Surely everyone will agree that a society is better when its citizens emphasize social responsibilities than when its citizens emphasize individual rights.

Humanists emphasize personal rights in the form of receiving social benefits derived from civil liberties.

---

5 Paul C. Vitz, *Psychology as Religion: The Cult of Self-Worship* (Grand Rapids: Wm. B. Erdman Publishing Company. 1977), 83.

Conclusion

The social values of Humanism are now gaining popularity in the Western World. Humanists are seeking the codification of their social values into law. If Christians want to retain benefits derived from legal status of Christian social values, then Christians must not only persuade individuals that Christian social values are superior but must also be legally and politically active in order to combat Humanist social influences.

Today the forces of social decomposition are challenging—and in some instances, overtaking—the forces of social composition. And when decomposition takes hold, it exacts an enormous human cost. Unless these exploding social pathologies are reversed, they will lead to the decline and perhaps even to the fall of the American republic.[1]

PLAYING WITH FIRE

Nichole and Justin were lovers, and they did not try to hide their relationship. After all, they were both 21. Nichole's dad confronted her: "Your lifestyle is wrong. You've no right to live with Justin until you are married."

"Dad, I know you don't approve, but what does a piece of paper have to do with anything? We are in love; we trust each other. Please don't bring up that God stuff again. *My* god wants me to be happy."

Her dad lowered his voice and put his arm around her. "Do you believe in the God that says 'the body is not for sexual immorality but for the Lord' and 'flee sexual immorality'? Do you believe in the God that warns all sexually immoral people that they will 'have their part in a lake which burns with fire and brimstone'? Is He your God?"

---

1 William J. Bennett, *The Index of Leading Cultural Indicators Facts and Figures on the State of American Society* (New York: Simon & Schuster: 1994), 8.

Nichole dropped her head. "Dad, I used to believe in that God, but he has become too rigid. *My* god isn't that way."

"You have changed, Nicole. The true God has not changed. You've created a god that pleases you but is unable to function on your behalf. Your god is nothing more than an idol. I pray God's mercy on you as you try to sort this out."

What are some of the results of creating a god to your liking?

Review Questions

1. Describe some differences in the philosophical foundations of Christian and Humanist views about sociology.

2. How does Christian thinking about sociology differ from Humanist thinking regarding the way individuals and societies are perceived?

3. Identify significant differences between Christian and Humanist thinking regarding family values.

4. How do Christians and Humanists differ regarding the way the church should function in society?

5. How do Christians and Humanists differ regarding the way the State should function in society?

6. How do Christians and Humanists differ in the perceptions of the nature of economics in society?

7. How do Christians and Humanists differ regarding how values should be taught within society?

8. Which social institution flourishes in a Christian society?

9. Which social institution dominates in a Humanist society?

10. In what ways may Christian social values be said to be superior to Humanist social values?

11. In which type society had you rather live: Christian or Humanist? Why? What can you do to insure your preference?

Suggested Readings in Sociology

Grant, George. *Bringing in the Sheaves: Transforming Poverty into Productivity*, Atlanta: American Vision Press, 1985.

Grant, George. *The Dispossessed: Homelessness in America*, Ft. Worth, TX: Dominion Press, 1986.

CHAPTER

LAW

Why have law and order deteriorated so rapidly in the United States? Simply because for many years it has been commonly taught that life is a random, accidental phenomenon with no meaning except the purely materialistic one. Laws are merely a matter of human expediency. Since humans are allegedly accidents, so are their laws.[1]

Laws are rules and regulations by which everyone in a particular society is expected to live. Christians and Humanists think differently about the source, authority, and purposes of law. The way people think about law determines the effectiveness of law in any given society. The results of law are therefore different, depending on whether law is considered from a Christian or from a Humanist perspective. These differences will be recognized, and then Christian perspectives about law will be shown superior to Humanist perspectives.

---

1 A. E. Wilder Smith, *The Creation of Life* (Costa Mesa, CA: TWFT Publishers, 1970), ix.

Contrasting Legal Differences

Legal Foundations

Christians think law is based on both general and special revelation; Humanists think law is based on human reason. General revelation refers to the many ways God reveals himself through his creation. Special revelation refers to the word of God as declared in the Bible. Natural law—general revelation—may be illustrated by the fact that every person has an inborn sense of right and wrong. For Christians, law requires people to abide by God's standards. For Humanists, law, while utilizing the sense of "ought" in people, allows people to determine their own laws apart from any considerations about God.

Humanists may arbitrarily accept or reject any laws they wish. They may agree with some aspects of God's commandment that "you shall not commit adultery"—thus rejecting rape—but at the same time permit promiscuous, pre-marital, and extra-marital sex—even incest! Humanists assume humans are capable of governing themselves by reason.

Humanists may agree to abide by God's commandment, "You shall not murder" but, at the same time they permit abortion.

Legal Functions

Christians believe God's word is the foundation for all law, so they emphasize law enforcement, not law making. When people know and respect God's law, they govern their own lives with little need for communal laws. However, Humanists believe humanity is the foundation for all law, so they emphasize making laws, not law enforcement. When people reject God's law, their governance requires that human laws must be imposed upon them by communal enactments.

LAW

Humanists believe law comes from humanity—they emphasize legislation. Christians believe law comes from God—they emphasize enforcement.

Legal Absolutes

Christians believe law is founded on God and his creation; it is constant and absolute. Humanists believe law is based on the theory of evolution and directed by human reasoning; it is always changing and relative. (This does not mean Christians cannot legislate but that laws Christians make must always conform to God's word.) Everyone can feel secure in a society whose laws are constant, but insecurity characterizes a society whose laws are always changing. In a Christian system of law, everyone can understand laws that are unchanging and absolute. When laws are constantly changing, as in Humanism, many may be confused about a disputable statute until judges determine its current meaning.

Since Christian laws are constant, everyone can know the meanings of legal statutes. For Humanists, laws evolve. Legal statutes do not necessarily mean what they say. They mean what the judges say they mean, and those stated meanings set precedents for the interpretation of the statutes in different contexts. Over time, laws evolve to meanings that differ from the original.

Fewer laws are needed in a society of Christians because citizens govern themselves by God's word.

Legal Purposes

Christians believe the purpose of law is to restrain evil and to promote righteousness according to biblical concepts of justice. Humanists believe the purpose of law is to direct public policies regarding acceptable human behavior according to Humanist precepts. Christians also believe law is intended to punish evil people and reward righteous individuals (Romans 13:4; 1 Peter 2:14) in keeping with God's declarations of good and evil. In contrast, Humanists believe law is intended to punish those who reject their public policies and reward those who practice their principles. For Christians, law requires the individual, the family, the church, and the nation to submit first to God (and only then to other authorities). For Humanists, law denies the existence of God and requires the individual, the family, and the church to submit to the State.

In a system of law based on Christian principles, God's word constitutes an absolute standard by which everybody—individually and collectively—is governed. Since there is self-government under God, there is limited and restricted civil government. However, in a system of law based on Humanist principles where all laws are relative and constantly changing, people have no constant and absolute standard by which to govern themselves. Therefore, for Humanists, civil government must be unlimited and unrestricted in its regulatory powers. Ideally, in law based on Humanism, the State must be democratic in order that the will of the majority may be established through the State. But that is theory—what actually happens in practice?

In practice, the State becomes the tool of special interest minority groups to wield control to their own advantage over the majority.

Criminal Punishment

Basically, this difference is related to disagreements regarding the nature of humanity. Christians consider people to be sinners; Humanists consider people to be basically good. For Christians, since people are responsible for their crime, confinement is—at least ideally—only until trial, after which punishment is inflicted upon the guilty. The Bible says nothing about imprisonment being imposed as a penalty for crime. Sometimes punishment is the death penalty. Old Testament law required that thieves restore stolen property to victims of their crimes (Exodus 22:1, 4). Biblical law emphasizes victims' rights.[1]

On the other hand, in a legal system consistent with Humanism, society and its environment—not individuals—are responsible for the existence of crime. Humanists generally think criminals should be rehabilitated, not punished. For Humanists, rehabilitation may require lengthy imprisonment, but never the death penalty because laws change, and what may be thought worthy of death at one time may not be so considered at another time. Convicted felons have their rights! Criminals repay their debt to society. Restitution is not awarded to victims. Since society is considered at fault for crimes by criminals, then society must pay for lengthy imprisonment of prisoners in order that criminals may no longer harm society.

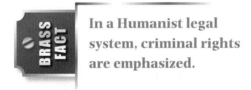

In a Humanist legal system, criminal rights are emphasized.

Methods for Changing Society

Because Christians recognize sin in everyone, they seek to improve society through motivating everyone to become better by conforming to biblical standards. A better society results from better individuals. On the other hand, Humanists believe Christian social standards are invalid because they are based on the character of God, a God that Humanists think does not exist. Humanists therefore seek to produce revolutionary social changes through legal and political procedures that include changing Christian beliefs and conduct about sex, marriage, and family.

---

1 For information about victim's rights in Scripture, read Gary North, *Victim's Rights: The Biblical View of Civil Justice* (Tyler, TX: Institute for Christian Economics), 1990.

CHRISTIANITY OR HUMANISM

LAW	Biblical Christianity	or	Secular Humanism
Foundation	God's word	or	Human reason
Perspective	Accepts only God's law	or	Arbitrarily accepts or rejects any legal policy or statute
Values	Emphasizes knowledge and enforcement of God's laws	or	Emphasizes legislation of laws, not law enforcement
Absolutes	God's law is considered constant and absolute.	or	Human law is considered flexible and relative.
Purpose	Restrains evil, promotes righteousness	or	Directs public policies according to contemporary perspective
Subjection	Submit first to God, then to governments	or	Individuals, families, and churches must submit to State
Government	Limited and restricted	or	Unlimited and unrestricted
Criminal Punishment	Individuals are responsible for their crimes	or	Society is responsible for crime
SUMMARY	God	or	Man

Why Christian Law Is Superior

It Produces Order

A legal system based on Humanist principles tends to produce social disorder and immorality. If law is sacred, as Christians consider it to be, then it is consistent and binding on everyone, because God is over all. On the other hand, if law is not sacred, then it is flexible and arbitrary, and no more binding than what is desirable or enforceable by the State. When law is considered sacred, to disobey law is to disobey God. Hence, in a society where God is respected, Christians revere law, and social order is maintained. However, when law is not considered sacred, to disobey law is to disobey only the State. Hence, in a society where God is rejected, and where communal laws constantly fluctuate, Humanists tend to disrespect law. The social order has no absolute moral foundation. Lawlessness and immorality, by Christian standards, are inevitable consequences of Humanism.

LAW

 Citizens give greater respect to law in a Christian society, thinking their laws come from God.

Universal Standard for Justice

Christian law alone provides a universal standard for ascertaining justice. A legal system based on precepts of Humanism may provide tentative standards for determining whether or not one has lived in conformity with its principles, but its precepts may not be just. When people look to God for an absolute and unchanging standard of conduct, they look to a standard above and beyond themselves. But when people look to the State for standards of conduct, they look only to arbitrary, relative, and changing standards that are no greater than the power of the State. These flexible standards may require temporary conformity, yet not provide justice. A Christian legal system is one of rule by law; a Humanist legal system is one of rule by men.

Human Rights and Responsibilities

Christian Law provides better human rights and demands greater responsibilities. Christians believe all rights come from God. Humanists believe all rights come from the State. For Christians, responsibilities are owed ultimately to God; for Humanists, responsibilities are owed ultimately to the State.

Just one example of differences in rights and responsibilities will illustrate how a Christian legal system is superior. Human rights under a Christian legal system are better because they guarantee the right to life from conception to the grave. Under a Humanist legal system, the right to life is accorded only to those who are desired or productive. Responsibilities under a Christian legal system require caring not only for self and family but also voluntary care of others. Under a Humanist legal system, care is not required of others, except as coerced through State taxation.

Conclusion

In the United States until the mid-1800s, law was generally based on principles of Christianity. Law was generally taught by using legal commentaries by William Blackstone (1723–1780), which were based on biblical precepts. However, with the coming of age of the theory of evolution (1859), the teaching of law changed. No longer is law taught as absolute. No longer is the teaching of law based upon the word of God. Now schools of law generally teach law as relative, based on the theory of evolution and executed by human reasoning. Because many Christian legal practitioners reject Humanist legal standards, the courts now give mixed judgments, sometimes from a Christian perspective, sometimes from a Humanist perspective. Individuals seeking justice in the courts are therefore concerned about whether judges and juries have a Christian or a Humanist worldview. We cannot yet know which legal perspective will eventually dominate and control the nation's legal system.

The creation of a pluralist society means the creation eventually of different laws for different groups and cultures within our nation, and indeed this is already happening with regard to some cultural groups. But even then, it must be understood that a pluralist society is not an end in itself, but simply a transitional phase, the crossing point of two cultures, in which the various contenders struggle for supremacy until one finally is victorious and proceeds to impose its culture and its law upon the rest of society. In that transformation our ideas of justice, based so firmly on Christian ideals, will be swept away and our nation will enter a new dark age.

The descent into such a dark age has already begun. Christian law is today being replaced by Humanistic law which does not recognize God or his law, nor the fundamental principles of justice set forth by that law and which have governed our law making and the development of our legal institutions for well over a millennium.[1]

---

1 Stephen C. Perks, *Christianity and Law: An Enquiry into the Influence of Christianity and the Development of English Common Law*, (Whitby, England: Avant Books, 1993), 55–56.

LAW

PLAYING WITH FIRE

Matt was only 31, a father, a history teacher, and a coach. His wife Erma was critically injured in the crash that took his life. Her legacy is a broken body and three children to rear, the oldest barely six. A witness to the accident said Matt's dying word was "Why?" His family is still asking that question.

Why was 24-year-old Ramon driving without a license? And why did his time in jail expire in less than a week after Matt's funeral? The greater question is, why hadn't Ramon been deported three years ago when his illegal immigration status was discovered when he was first arrested for drunk driving—with an alcohol level three times the legal limit?

Matt was killed by an illegal alien with five previous DUI arrests on his record.

Why indeed?

For Humanists, laws evolve—legal statutes do not necessarily mean what they say. **How does this example illustrate that statement?**

Review Questions

1. How do Christians and Humanists differ in their thinking about philosophical foundations of law?

2. Define the following terms: natural law, biblical law, natural rights, civil rights.

3. Identify significant differences between Christian and Humanist legal precepts.

4. How do Christians and Humanists differ in their thinking about law enforcement?

5. How do Christians and Humanists differ in their views of crime and punishment?

6. How do Christian and Humanist legal systems differ in their results?

7. Why do you think a system of law based on Christian precepts is superior to a system of law based on Humanist precepts?

8. What legal changes have you observed in your lifetime that lead you to believe our laws are changing from Christian foundations to Humanist foundations?

9. What can you do to reverse the escalation of a legal system based on Humanism?

Suggested Readings in Law

Barton, David. *Original Intent: The Courts, the Constitution, and Religion* (Aledo, TX: WallBuilder Press), 1997.

North, Gary. *Victim's Rights: The Biblical View of Civil Justice* (Tyler, TX: Institute for Christian Economics), 1990.

Perks, Stephen. *Christianity and Law: An Enquiry into the Influence of Christianity on the Development of English Common Law* (Whitby, England: Avant Books), 1993.

Rushdoony, Rousas John. *The Institutes of Biblical Law*, Vol. 1 (Presbyterian and Reformed Publishing Company), 1973.

Whitehead, John W. *The Second American Revolution* (Elgin, IL: David C. Cook Publishing Co.), 1982.

CHAPTER 10

POLITICS

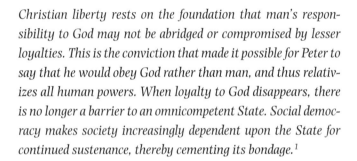

Christian liberty rests on the foundation that man's responsibility to God may not be abridged or compromised by lesser loyalties. This is the conviction that made it possible for Peter to say that he would obey God rather than man, and thus relativizes all human powers. When loyalty to God disappears, there is no longer a barrier to an omnicompetent State. Social democracy makes society increasingly dependent upon the State for continued sustenance, thereby cementing its bondage.[1]

Politics is the management of government, especially of civil government. Since many people generally are not accustomed to thinking of politics as being either Christian or Humanist, then, for them, differences in religious political perspectives may be a new approach to understanding contemporary politics. Differences in Christian and Humanist political perspectives will first be observed, then reasons will be given to demonstrate why, in politics, the Christian worldview is superior to the Humanist worldview.

---

1 Herbert Schlossberg, *Idols for Destruction: Christian Faith and Its Confrontation with American Society*, (Nashville: Thomas Nelson Publishers, 1983), 229.

Contrasting Political Worldviews

Philosophical Foundations of Politics

Christian thought about politics is based upon Christian perception of law, which is based upon Christian ethics, which is based upon the righteous character of God. Humanist thought about politics is based upon Humanist perception of law, which is based upon Humanist ethics, which is based upon the presumed goodness of mankind. Because Christian perception of politics is derived ultimately from the unchanging character of God, then Christian political perspective has a uniform and constant standard by which it can operate. On the other hand, because Humanist perception of politics is derived ultimately from various individual determinations of what constitutes right and wrong, then Humanist political perspective has no uniform and consistent standard by which it can operate.

 Humanist political policy is inconsistent—it comes from the changing ideologies of humanity.

Political Beliefs

Christians believe that God assigns to civil governments the role and responsibility of administering justice in society, and that the powers of civil governments are limited by God to whatever he has authorized in Scripture. "Whatever you do in word or deed, do all in the name of the Lord Jesus" (Colossians 3:17).

Christian politics include these convictions:

1. Since everyone is a sinner, less evil will be administered in civil government when the governing powers are distributed among all people, because there will be less potential for a few to impose power on the many.

2. People should govern themselves individually and collectively by the word of God, and governing powers are more accountable to the people when they are localized. A government that contends that God sanctions its politics should affirm that its rule and moral order are based on God's character—holiness, justice, love, mercy, truth—and that people are created in God's image. Such a government also affirms that everyone sins, that individuals have great worth, and that God judges everyone's behavior.

3. The governance of church and family, when based on Christian law, should be outside of political considerations of civil governments, except when related to justice.

Humanist politics embrace the following ideals:

1. People assign to civil governments the role and responsibilities of regulating all individual and institutional human behavior. People, not God, limit the powers of civil governments.

2. Since all people are considered to be basically good, the best and wisest of mankind should rule over the rest of mankind.

3. Governing powers should be centralized, elitist, and bureaucratic by human legislative standards.

A government that contends that only people authorize its politics is likely to affirm that God is non-existent and irrelevant. It is also inclined to insist that the moral order should be based on the will of the people, that human beings evolve, that man is basically good, that the State is of superior worth, and that human beings are accountable only to mankind, that is, to the State. Humanists generally contend that governance of church and family should be based on Humanist law, and therefore included within all political considerations.

The Proper Functional Role of Politics

Christians seek an ideological union of Christian religion, with but a functional separation from civil government. Humanists seek an ideological separation of Christian religion from civil government, with civil government regulating religion. In other words, Christian politics ideally requires that civil authorities not only believe in the existence of God and hold to biblical values but also that politics be administered by Christian principles. Christian politics does not authorize the church to function in the administration of civil justice.

Christians contend that the role of the church is to teach the word of God regarding the administration of justice—that the function of civil government is to administer civil justice based on biblical precepts. Christians do not endorse a formal administrative union of church and State because such is not taught in Scripture. Christians do, however, call for an ideological union between the Christian religion and civil government, inasmuch as all law is based on religion.

 If law and politics are not based on the Christian religion, they will be based on some other religion.

Humanist politics seeks to void all influence of Christian religion in the political arena. Humanists do not want Christian ideology to influence politics in any way. If Humanists can eliminate Christian religion from politics, then they can dominate the political arena by their own ideology and activity. They deceptively call for the "separation of church and State," by which they mean separation of Christian religion from civil government. Humanists want law and politics to be administered by the religious values of Humanism, even though they are generally unwilling to declare Humanism a religion.

Political Goals

Christians support separation of civil governments, that is, separate nations. Humanists seek a single global government. Christians desire that all nations operate by biblical principles; Humanists desire a single, federated, world government based on the will of all people. To accomplish their goals, Christians generally support private ownership and regulation of property, and voluntary economic help to assist poor individuals and nations. But Humanists, to accomplish their goals, generally seek public ownership and regulation of property, and redistribution of wealth through taxation and distributive welfare programs.

POLITICS	Biblical Christianity	or	Secular Humanism
Foundation	God's word		Human declarations
Perspective	Consistent operational standards	or	Standards vary with human desires
Organization	Governing powers are distributed; civil governments are under God's authority.	or	Governing power is centralized and elitist; bureaucrats rule, supposedly under the will of the people.
Values	Everyone sins; behavior is accountable to both God and mankind.	or	Everyone is basically good; behavior is accountable only to other people.
Purpose	Christian values unite family, church, and state with God's word regulating all aspects of life.	or	Secular values unite family and state with state regulating all aspects of life.
Goals	Nationalism, private ownership, and regulation of property; benevolence is voluntary.	or	One-world government; public ownership and regulation of property; redistribution of wealth
Realities	Small governments; family growth and social stability	or	Large governments; state growth and social instability
SUMMARY	God	or	Man

Why Christian Politics Is Superior

Consistency with Natural, Social, and Economic Realities

A Christian system is more consistent with natural, social, and economic realities. A Christian political system operating in harmony with Christian sociology recognizes the family as the basic unit of society. Since the only biblical declarations regarding the purpose of civil governments is for the administration of justice (which includes maintaining peace and insuring public safety), a Christian political system would encourage stability and growth of the family while keeping civil government small.

1. Ideally, to aid in keeping the family as the basic unit in society, a Christian political system would not tax families for purposes other than for the administration of civil justice.

2. Families would be required to provide for themselves and for their extended family members (1 Timothy 5:8), rather than receive provisions from the State.

3. People would be allowed to retain and use the economic fruits of their own labors, rather than allowing politicians to collect and redistribute the peoples' wealth in order to buy votes and thereby retain political power.

A political system operating in harmony with Humanist sociology makes the individual the basic unit of society. This it does by the authority of the State, as determined by changing Humanist values.

1. A Humanist system encourages the growth of the State, and thereby makes a god of the State.

2. Rather than expecting the family to provide for its own, Humanist politics declares that the State should provide for its citizens.

3. Humanist politics seeks a worldwide form of taxation of individuals and corporations to support needs of citizens in all nations.

Individual and Religious Freedom

A Christian political system grants more individual and religious freedoms. A Christian system leaves individuals free to live as they choose within the parameters of Christian law. While individuals must abide by Christian law, they are free not to believe in God or other Christian values. On the other hand, while Humanist politics claims to seek greater freedom for individuals, Humanists really mean freedom from God. A Humanist system literally enslaves individuals to governance by the State. Individuals must not only abide by Humanist law, they must also accept other Humanist values.

A Humanist political system operates by multiple, inconsistent, and human-derived ethical standards; each person determines his own values.

Absolute Precepts

A Christian political system is based on absolute precepts given by God in Scripture. Scripture declares that the purpose of civil government is to administer justice—righteousness—by punishing the evil and rewarding the righteous (Romans 13:4; 1 Peter 2:14). Since a Christian political system is at least ideally consistent because it is based on the unchanging word of God, is it not reasonable to conclude that it will surely produce a consistent judicial process? But a political system like Humanism is inherently inconsistent.

By using absolute precepts, citizens have consistent standards by which they may evaluate political policies and procedures. Citizens who elect their governing officials can hold them accountable to absolute standards or vote them out of office. Because a Christian political system is based on absolutes, it allows citizenry to have a greater sense of confidence in the political system. A Christian political system has a definite and absolute ethical system by which its politics can operate.

Humanists have no absolute standard, so they cannot teach values that hinder an avalanche of crime and immorality.

A Humanist political system generally cannot operate by any common standard of ethics, because each person determines his or her own ethical system. Ethical values in a Humanist political system are constantly changing because they are based on evolutionary presuppositions. These changing ethical considerations in politics produce civil confusion and instability.

Less Crime

A Christian political system produces societies in which there is less crime. A Christian society has an absolute standard: it teaches its citizens—primarily through the family structure—Christian values such as love toward God and fellowman. It teaches courtesy, manners, personal integrity and accountability, sanctity of life, respect for law and authority, marital commitment, moral purity, the spiritual nature of mankind, and the certainty of an eternal judgment.

Christian values contribute toward a reduction of crime and greater personal safety.

Conclusion

Currently, politics in the Unites States is generally not regulated by Christian values but by values of Humanism. Many politicians now give greater emphasis to economic and educational interests than to the administration of justice. Many seem more interested in seeking personal political power than in seeking righteousness in their societies. Christians should give greater consideration to the nature and functions of politics, and then, whenever possible, speak and act according to Christian principles in the political arena.

People who have experienced liberty often require strong motivation to give it up. Those who wish to impose State power on them provide the strongest reason of all for doing so: salvation from disaster, named or unnamed . . . The second Humanist Manifesto declares that we cannot survive without "bold and daring" measures, by which it means collectivist ones. Those who can be convinced that survival is at stake are likely to agree to almost anything, since extinction seems worse than all the alternatives. If placing extraordinary powers in the hands of political leaders will truly stave off the ultimate disaster, then those who demur can be made to appear as enemies of the human race. That is why arguments based on survival are so effective in persuading people to permit actions that violate their moral code.[1]

---

1 Herbert Schlossberg, *Idols for Destruction: Christian Faith and Its Confrontation with American Society* (Nashville: Thomas Nelson Publishers, 1983), 180–181.

CHRISTIANITY OR HUMANISM

PLAYING WITH FIRE

Money talks. Who would know that better than software mogul Leonard Lull, the wealthy homosexual activist? In one year he targeted 70 state-level races in more than a dozen states. And he was only one of several who funneled millions of dollars into dozens of carefully selected campaigns of candidates who favored same-sex marriage.

Lull's staff confirmed his launching of an "under-the-radar political giving campaign." It is no secret that Leonard can spot pro-family lawmakers who support state marriage amendments and woo them with big bucks. Yes, money talks.

Inspired by the example of Lull, philanthropist Florida billionaire Cal Clyker openly boasts that he is contributing heavily "to elect gay-friendly governors and state lawmakers." He sees nothing wrong with being a powerful outside influence in local and state elections.

Is a local farmer in Mississippi going to be pleased to know that his pro-family representative was unseated by a homosexual stealth money strategy? How do Americans in general feel about these activists? Most of them are ignorant of the work of such activists. Homosexuals tend to have a great deal of disposable time and money for political activity, because they do not have children and their partners often provide them with a second income. And that money has an agenda.

Money talks to politicians.

If Christian activists were employing the above strategy to influence the political arena, would the mainstream media be wringing their hands in frustration? How does this relate to Humanism and Christianity?

Review Questions

1. What constitutes the philosophical foundations for politics in the Christian system?
2. What constitutes the philosophical foundations for politics in the Humanist system?
3. How do Christians and Humanists differ in their political assumptions and affirmations?
4. How do Christian and Humanists differ in their political affirmations about the nature of civil governments?
5. How do Christians and Humanists differ in their political objectives?
6. How do Christians and Humanists differ in the political understandings about "church and State"?
7. In what ways may a Christian political system claim to be superior to a Humanist political system?
8. How do you suppose politicians would act different from what you think they now do if they all operated politically from a Christian perspective?
9. How can you change current political practices and make them more consistent with the Christian worldview?

Suggested Readings in Politics

Barton, David. *The Myth of Separation*, Aledo, TX: WallBuilder Press, 1989.

DeMar, Gary. *Ruler of the Nations: Biblical Principles for Government*, Ft. Worth, TX: Dominion Press, 1987.

Eidsmoe, John. *God and Caesar: Christian Faith and Political Action*. Westchester, IL: Crossway Books, 1984

Jordan, James B. *Judges: God's War against Humanism*, Tyler, TX: Geneva Ministries, 1985.

North, Gary. *Political Polytheism: The Myth of Pluralism*, Tyler, TX: Institute for Christian Economics, 1989.

Sutton, Ray. *Who Owns the Family: God or the State?* Ft. Worth, TX: Dominion Press, 1986.

Woods, Dennis. *Discipling the Nations: The Government upon His Shoulder*, Franklin, TN: Legacy Communications, 1996.

CHAPTER

11

ECONOMICS

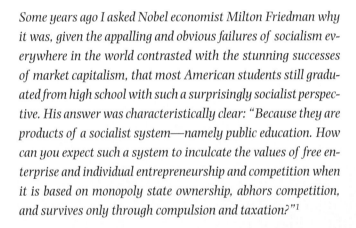

Some years ago I asked Nobel economist Milton Friedman why it was, given the appalling and obvious failures of socialism everywhere in the world contrasted with the stunning successes of market capitalism, that most American students still graduated from high school with such a surprisingly socialist perspective. His answer was characteristically clear: "Because they are products of a socialist system—namely public education. How can you expect such a system to inculcate the values of free enterprise and individual entrepreneurship and competition when it is based on monopoly state ownership, abhors competition, and survives only through compulsion and taxation?"[1]

Historically, the development of political economic systems is comparatively recent in world history. The free enterprise system of economics, also called capitalism, developed from the thinking of Adam Smith (1723–1790), who is generally regarded as the founder of modern political economic theory. In 1776, his economic theory was published in a book titled *An Inquiry into the Nature and Causes of the Wealth of Nations*.

An opposing economic theory, usually designated as socialism, was formulated by Karl Marx (1818–1883) and published in *Das*

---

1 Warren T. Brookes, "Public Education and the Global Failure of Socialism," *Imprimis*, XIX, 4, (1990), 1.

Kapital. The first volume was printed in 1867; the second and third volumes were published posthumously in 1885 and 1894.

The Bible does not specify any particular economic system for a nation, although it does present economic principles, especially for individuals. Biblical economic principles are more compatible with capitalism than with any other economic system, although capitalism is not always consistent with Christian principles. Nor should Christians necessarily consider themselves capitalists.

Not all Humanists consider themselves socialists, but socialism comes closest to characterizing Humanist principles of political economics. (Communism, fascism, and democratic socialism are but varied forms of socialism, all of which are greatly imbued to various degrees with the Humanist worldview.) Because capitalism is more akin to Christian thought, and socialism is more in tune with Humanist ideology, contrasting Christian and Humanist economical ideals is at least partially a contrast between capitalism and socialism.

Contrasting Economic Worldviews

Production and Distribution of Wealth

Capitalism relies on private ownership of property; socialism relies on public ownership. This means that in capitalism, individuals work for their own benefit and then spend the fruits of their labor as they choose. In socialism, people labor to create wealth for the State, which then spends it as it chooses—ideally to disperse it equally among its citizens.

Humanists believe an elite civil group has the right to plan for everyone.

ECONOMICS

The Nature of Humanity

While Christians believe people sin, Humanists consider mankind perfectible and basically good. If people are sinners, the best economic system is one wherein civil government impartially protects human rights, and where individuals may enjoy the fruits of their labors. However, if people are basically good, then from a Humanist perspective, the best economic system is one wherein the State assures equality in production and distribution of wealth.

> If people are sinners, then civil government must protect prosperity of individuals who work for their wealth by punishing those who steal.

The Existence of Prosperity and Poverty

Christians believe national prosperity comes from peoples' obedience to God's work ethic. Humanists believe prosperity comes from economic planning by the State.

The Management of Wealth

Christians believe each individual has the right to plan and execute his or her own economic affairs. Humanists believe an elite group in the State has the right to plan economics for everyone within society.

Christians depend primarily upon nuclear and extended families, and secondarily upon the church and community volunteers for financial support of individuals unable to care for themselves. Humanists depend upon civil governments to provide for the needs of individuals.

Christians reason that Humanism makes people dependent upon the State (not God), and that socialism tends toward indolence rather than industry. Humanists think that the free market system of capitalism is uncontrollable and therefore intolerable, since mankind (via the State) is thought needful to guide and control everything.

BRASS FACT: Christians believe prosperity comes from obedience to God's work ethic; Humanists believe prosperity comes from economic planning by civil governments.

Production and Distribution of Wealth

Capitalism expects the market to be free from State regulation because it trusts the free market place and depends upon individuals and families to plan and execute their own economic welfare. But socialism requires vast State bureaucracies. It depends upon centralized control by an elite group within the State to plan and execute economic welfare for all of society.

Capitalism is essentially not so much concerned with money but with human freedom and responsibility. It expects the State to administer justice. Socialism is essentially concerned with the State's control of the economy—not with personal freedom and responsibility. Christians believe prosperity comes from obedience to God's work ethic. Why do they desire capitalism? Because, without State collectivism, people have incentive to work for the fruits of their own labors. But Humanists believe that prosperity comes from the State's economic planning. They generally desire socialism because they think it will lead ultimately to a centralized and productive global economy.

Possession of Property

Christians believe "the earth is the Lord's and the fullness thereof" (Psalm 24:1), that human beings are only temporary stewards of property. Humanists believe all property is presumably owned by the State. That is why supposedly "private" property is taxable by the State.

ECONOMICS

Ethical Economic Principles

For Christians, ethical economic principles are determined by God and revealed in Scripture. At least two biblical ethical principles favor capitalism. One is "if any will not work neither should he eat" (2 Thessalonians 3:10). The other is "you shall not steal" (Exodus 20:15). The latter is also a rejection of socialism because it denies the right of the State to take unduly from individuals—as Ahab took Naboth's vineyard (1 Kings 21:1–14)—even if legalized through taxation. For Humanists, ethical economic principles are determined by the fact that the State is considered the highest authority. Since in Humanism all things are considered relative, then the State determines ethical economic practices—however much they may change—for civil governments as well as for individuals.

Economic Authority of the State

Christian economics holds individuals and families responsible for administering economic welfare, education, and health care. Churches may also volunteer to assist in these areas. Christian economics does not consider the State as having biblical authority for these functions. Humanist economics, however, holds that the State is essentially responsible for economic, educational, and health care of its citizens. In fact, for Humanists, the State must function in these areas in order to achieve socialism, egalitarianism, multiculturalism, and political globalism.

ECONOMICS	Biblical Christianity	or	Secular Humanism
Production of Wealth	Individuals work, earn, and spend as they choose.	or	Individuals work for the state, then receive redistribution of wealth.
Human Nature	People sin; some steal; governments protect human property rights.	or	People are good; state assures equality in productivity and wealth.
Prosperity	Derived from God's work ethic; requires individual and family industriousness	or	Derived from state planning and redistribution of wealth
Principles	If any will not work, neither should he eat.	or	State determines all economic policies and practices.
State Authority	Individuals, families, and churches administer welfare, education, health care, etc.	or	State is responsible for economic, education, and health care, etc.
SUMMARY	God	or	Man

Why Christian Economics Is Superior

It Creates Greater Wealth and Prosperity

National economics based upon obedience to God is greater than national economics that is not based on obedience to God (Deuteronomy 7:12–15; 28:1–8). Because an ideal Christian economical system would not be regulated by the State, individuals would have personal freedom, independence, and incentive to work for greater personal wealth, and therefore produce greater personal, family, and national prosperity.

However, a Humanist economical system, based on heavy taxation and redistribution of wealth, takes away work incentives and creates economic dependency. A Humanist economical system ends in individual economic slavery to the State. Surely all will agree that the economic system that produces greater personal, family, and national prosperity, as well as economic freedom, is the better economic system.

It Grants Greater Personal Economic Freedoms

Freedom comes as a result of assuming responsibility. A Christian economical system allows greater independence and requires self-reliance. A Christian economical system gives greater authority to individuals and families, and thereby limits the authority of the State. It places economic responsibility on individuals and families, rather than conditioning people to demand economic rights or entitlements from civil government.

BRASS FACT Christian economics includes voluntary and unselfish sharing of one's goods with others.

Conclusion

Christian economic ideals in the form of capitalism now appear to be fading in civil governments. Humanist economics in the form of socialism now dominates State-directed economic welfare programs. However, a Christian system of economics is more than capitalism, and therefore should not be exclusively identified with it. Christian economics includes voluntarily and unselfishly sharing of one's goods with others. "Let him who stole steal no longer, but rather let him labor, working with his hands what is good, that he may have something to give him who has need" (Ephesians 4:28). The Christian understands that "it is more blessed to give than to receive" (Acts 20:35). Christians are to give liberally (Romans 12:8). Therefore, "as we have opportunity, let us do good to all, especially to those who are of the household of faith" (Galatians 6:10).

Just before the collapse of socialism in the Soviet bloc, Lutheran sociologist Peter Berger wrote a marvelous book about the newly industrializing countries of East Asia. These "little tigers," or "little dragons" as they're sometimes called, are part of a capitalist revolution and, as Berger documents, they are defeating poverty at an amazing rate. He compares them to the Third World nations that have tried socialism for the last three decades and finds that none of the latter have grown, and indeed, that most have moved backward.[1]

PLAYING WITH FIRE

Dr. Baranski began his lecture. "Today, let's take a tour of the ideal system of government. In communism, everyone contributes into the system and everyone has access to needed goods and services. That system is best."

Jim Austin raised his hand: "Dr. Baranski, when the Soviet Union fell in 1991, it was in the heart of its fourth generation of citizens. If communism is so great, why the collapse?"

"Mr. Austin, you have introduced the greatest institution known to this date. Soviet citizens were secure: they were protected from internal and external forces. They enjoyed health care, rest, and relaxation. Was communism perfect? No. And thus her demise."

Jim Austin persisted: "What are some of her imperfections?"

"Mr. Austin, consider yourself, Miss Jones, and Mr. Deans. Each of you owns a car. Now put your heads together quickly and determine how many hours you use your cars in a week."

After a brief conference, Jim replied, "Dr. Baranski, we use our cars a total of 27 hours."

"If the three of you used a single car from a motor pool, and if six others also used that same car, it would still be idle more than half the time! Capitalism is wasteful."

"But, sir," Jim retorted. "Mr. Deans and I drive from our jobs to this class. And on weekends, all three of us each drive to separate destinations. We cannot use the same car, to say nothing of sharing it with six others."

Dr. Baranski smiled: "Ah-ha. Now we're at the root of the problem, class. Mr. Austin has not considered public transportation or

---

1 K. E. Grubbs, Jr., "A New 'Liberation Theology' for the World: Faith and the Free Market," *Impimis*, March, 1991, 4.

ECONOMICS

carpooling. He is thinking only of himself. The great Soviet Union had just enough of Mr. Austin's selfish spirit to destroy it.

"The solution? Maybe in another million years of continuing evolution, mankind will advance enough to get rid of its selfishness. Then what is left of our natural resources can be preserved and mankind will find true peace and contentment."

Is it wise for us to rely on evolution to solve our problems? What complications might be created if we rely on this Humanistic view of ecomonics?

Review Questions

1. Define capitalism and socialism.
2. How does the role of the civil government regarding economics differ when operating from Christian principles rather than from Humanist principles?
3. How does whether or not a civil government considers people sinners influence that government's attitude toward economics?
4. What is the correlation between capitalism and Christianity? What is the correlation between socialism and Humanism?
5. How do capitalists and socialists view each other's economic systems?
6. How does Christian economic theory regarding property differ from Humanist economic theory?
7. Describe some ethical values related to Christian economics? To Humanist economics?
8. How does the authority for State regulation of welfare, education, and health differ between Christian and Humanist economics?

9. In what ways may Christian economics be said to be superior to Humanist economics?

10. How would your personal economic situation differ if your civil government operated altogether by Christian economic principles? How can you change your civil government so that it does operate more by Christian economic principles?

Suggested Reading in Economics

Heilbroner, Robert L. *The Worldly Philosophers: The Lives, Times, and Ideas of the Great Economic Thinkers*, New York: Touchstone, 1999.

CHAPTER 12

EDUCATION

In most countries today, and no less in the United States, Humanism is the established religion of the State and is progressively the source of legal revisionism. Humanism is also the established religion of schools and most churches, and most of society. Christianity is quite logically progressively excluded from state, school, and church and has a weak and scarcely tenable position in modern life. It probably lacks extensive and organized persecution in most countries because orthodox Christianity has become progressively weaker and less and less relevant.[1]

Compulsory public education, supervised by civil governments, originated in many Western countries during the early nineteenth century. From its inception, it was dominated by the ideals of secularism and statism. The Unitarians and Horace Mann started the process in the USA in the early 1800s. In the late nineteenth century, John Dewey redesigned America's public schools to conform to philosophical foundations and psychological methodologies of what later came to be recognized as the Humanist worldview.[2]

---

[1] Rousas John Rushdoony, *Christianity and the State* (Vallecito, CA: Ross House Books, 1986), 8.

[2] Samuel L. Blumenfeld has written two excellent books regarding the background of the Stated directed public education system in the United States. They are *N. E. A.: Trojan Horse In American Education* (Boise, ID:

When government-supervised education began, the nation had a Christian social and cultural foundation. After nearly two centuries, public education, having operated under State control and based on Humanist ideology, is largely responsible for the removal of Christian values from the nation's social and cultural foundations. Christians need to understand not only the values of Humanism but also how Humanism operates in their civil governments' compulsory educational systems.[1] After differences are presented in educational worldviews of Christians and Humanists (regarding their aims, contents, methods, results, and authority), reasons will be given to show that Christian education is superior to Humanist education.

 Public education, based on Humanist ideology, is largely responsible for removing Christian values from our social and cultural foundations.

Contrasting Educational Worldviews

Educational Aims

Values that Christian education aims to promote include the knowledge of God, biblical understandings of human relationships to both God and man, insistence upon acceptance of both special and natural revelation, human submission to God, biblical morality, and self-government according to God's word. Christians aim to educate both the physical and spiritual natures of mankind.

Humanist education aims to promote the secularization and socialization of children (i.e., to teach children how to be socialists),

---

The Paradigm Co.) 1984, and *Is Public Education Necessary?* (Boise, ID: The Paradigm Co.) 1985.

1 See Kathleen M. Gow, *Yes, Virginia, There is Right and Wrong* (Wheaton, IL: Tyndale House Publishers), 1985; and Noebel, David A., J. F. Baldwin, and Kevin Bywater, *Clergy in the Classroom: The Religion of Secular Humanism* (Manitou Springs, CO: Summit Press), 1995.

rejection of supernaturalism, and insistence upon the naturalness, equality, and self-sufficiency of mankind. Other Humanist values promoted include materialism, feminism, relativism, hedonism, multiculturalism, and so forth. Humanists aim to educate only the physical nature of mankind because it believes human beings have neither a spiritual nature nor a possibility for eternal existence.

Christians and Humanists have different understandings about the role of teachers in the accomplishment of their respective objectives. In Christian education, teachers are considered instructors to impart knowledge, but in Humanist education, they are considered facilitators. Different understandings also exist regarding the roles of schools in society. In Christian education, schools are considered as extensions of the home; in Humanist education, schools are considered as extensions of the State.

Curriculum Content

For Christians, the Christian religion is foundational to life. Every field of study will encompass the Christian religion. Education must be not only religious but also specifically Christian. But Humanism permits a plurality of values and claims to be value neutral; Humanists insist that no single standard of values exists by which any academic or disciplinary study must be guided.

In making this claim, Humanists are inconsistent, because for Humanists, education must be altogether secular and secularism is a single standard. By insisting on secular education, Humanists demand that education exclude religion, meaning especially the Christian religion.

Christians and Humanists differ in their understanding of the fundamental foundation of education. For Christians, the foundation of knowledge and wisdom is God: "The fear of the Lord is the beginning of knowledge" (Proverbs 1:7). "The Lord gives wisdom" (Proverbs 2:6; James 1:5). Since God created the heavens and the earth (Genesis 1:1), then, for Christians, the doctrine of creation is the key to all knowledge and wisdom. However, for Humanists, the curriculum foundation is the theory of evolution. It is the key to all knowledge for Humanists. Every educational discipline in American public education must at least acknowledge the validity of the theory of evolution.

Moreover, Christian and Humanist education differ in their emphasis. Christian education emphasizes personal obedience, duty, and responsibility; Humanist education emphasizes moral autonomy and personal rights.

 For Christians, education must be not only religious but also specifically Christian, but for Humanists, education must be altogether secular.

Educational Methods

Consistent with the Christian understanding of the existence of God and absolute values, Christians are inclined to use the processes of didactic instruction, memorization, and recitation to achieve student learning of a body of knowledge. On the other hand, consistent with the Humanist conviction of the supremacy of mankind and of relative values, Humanists are inclined to use the processes of affective and subjective learning, along with behavioral modification and psychological manipulation to facilitate students' discovery of knowledge.

Another difference is that Christian educational methodology recognizes that teachers must know their subjects thoroughly. It allows teachers to be authoritarian in their discipline of students; they may use corporal punishment when needed. Humanist educational methodology declares that since teachers are primarily facilitators, their knowledge of their subjects needs not be so thorough. They must generally be permissive and without disciplinary authority.

Christian education requires a body of material to be learned; students are not promoted to the next grade level until the material in the present level is mastered. Humanist education does not generally require that a body of material be learned—only discovered! Then students are often automatically promoted regardless of subject matter mastery.

History indicates that when Christian values dominate, educational quality is excellent, but when Humanist values dominate, educational quality is only mediocre.

Desired Educational Results

Simply put, the desired result of Christian education is a society with Christian values. The desired result of Humanist education is a world of Humanist values. The results of different types of education are much more than that, however. History indicates that when Christian values dominated, educational quality in the United States was excellent. The adult illiteracy rate for Anglo-Saxons in the 1800s was 0.04 percent. In the 1930s, it was 1.5 percent. Moral character was strong. Children were expected to achieve greater things than their parents. Schools reinforced Christian values and character qualities. Children were generally well behaved.

Now that Humanist values dominate the national education system, educational quality is mediocre. Adult illiteracy rate for all segments in society now fluctuates at about 20 percent, while another 40 percent are barely literate.[1] Moral character is weak. Children are not expected to achieve anything equal to their parents. Government schools damage Christian values and character qualities. Students are often rowdy and sometimes violent.

---

[1] For an analysis of the literacy problem in America, read Rudolf Flesch, *Why Johnny Can't Read* (New York: Harper and Row), 1955, and *Why Johnny Still Can't Read* (New York: Harper and Row), 1981.

Educational Authority

Christian educational authority requires that, since parents are responsible for bringing up their children in the nurture and admonition of the Lord (Ephesians 6:1–4), then parents are altogether responsible for the nature, extent, and quality of their own children's education. In a fully Christian society, only private Christian schools, including home schools, could exist, and would be funded by parents or by charities for those unable to pay their own way.

Humanist educational authority requires that since the civil government is thought to be responsible for the education of children, then the State is responsible for the nature, extent, and quality of education given to children.[1] In a fully Humanist society, only schools that are regulated by civil governments could exist, and would be funded by taxes from the general population. Humanist education assumes that children and property belong first to the State, and only afterward to parents. It assumes the State has a right to compel children to attend school, and a right to require citizens to pay taxes for educational purposes.

---

1 For further information, see Adams, Blair and Joel Stein, *Who Owns the Children? Compulsory Education and the Dilemma of Ultimate Authority* (Grand Junction, CO: Truth Forum, 1983).

EDUCATION

EDUCATION	Biblical Christianity	or	Secular Humanism
Foundation	Standards set by God's laws; operates under His value system	or	Standards set by human policies, operates under state control
Knowledge	"The fear of the Lord is the beginning of knowledge."	or	The theory of evolution is the key to all knowledge.
Curriculum	Every field of study encompasses Christian values.	or	Every field of study encompasses pluralistic values
Purpose	Promotes biblical morality, submission, and knowledge of God's way of life	or	Promotes naturalism, materialism, secularism, multiculturalism, feminism, hedonism, socialism, etc.
Educational Authority	The family	or	The State
Teacher Functions	To impart knowledge; to promote godly morality, personal discipline.	or	To facilitate; be change-agents, promote humanist values
Instructional Methods	Teach absolute values by didactic instruction, memorization, recitation. Require learning.	or	Use subjective learning, behavioral modification, psychological manipulation. Encourage discovery.
SUMMARY	God	or	Man

Why Christian Education Is Superior

Greater Moral Results

Christian education trains both physical and spiritual aspects of human nature; therefore, it produces a moral sense that promotes greater personal integrity, service, and submission to rightful authority. These personal qualities create safer communities because people not only fear God and human authorities, but they also have more care and concern for each other.

Humanist education considers that human beings are only physical; so Humanist education produces selfishness and the implementation of the evolutionary idea of natural selection that translates into presumed rightfulness of the survival of the fittest.

The presumption that "might makes right" allows for intimidating, if not demolishing, the weak.

Greater Intellectual Results

Because Christian education requires mastery of a body of knowledge based on special and natural revelation, it is able to attain greater productivity that in turn creates greater prosperity. Furthermore, highly educated individuals are often more interested in service to humanity than in material prosperity.

A Life Base

It requires that the Christian religion be seen not just as part of life but as the foundation upon which all life is based. Christian education does not departmentalize life into categories of the secular and the sacred. It recognizes that all education is religious education because all education is based on religious assumptions of truth, virtue, and goodness. When education excludes religion, as Humanist education attempts to do, it implies—contrary to Scripture—the following concepts:

1. Religion is but a part of life and is not important.
2. God is not relevant to life.
3. People are judges of all things.

An Awareness of Eternity

Christian education recognizes that human beings are spiritual as well as physical, and that the spiritual nature of humanity lives on after separation from the physical body. It acknowledges that individuals are created in the image of God, must serve God, and will be judged by God. Christian education therefore causes people to act like they have an eternal destiny, either to heaven for having lived a life of obedient faith or to hell for having lived a faithless life of disobedience and rebellion against God.

EDUCATION

 Once schools were private; now they are public, operating by State taxes, under State control, and primarily by Humanist values.

Conclusion

Unlike secular education, Christian education encompasses all aspects of life. It produces better moral conduct and greater intellectual results, and it provides a constant awareness of eternal realities. Schools in the United States were once private, operating in the free market system, and primarily by Christian values in aims, curriculum content, methodology, and results. They are now public, that is, operating by State taxes, under State control, and primarily by Humanist values. That's because American public schools were designed by Horace Mann, John Dewey, and others—all with Humanistic values.

This means that if Christian parents provide their children with educational experiences consistent with Christian values, they cannot do so through government tax-supported schools. Humanist education will not only weaken or destroy Christian faith but also will weaken the church. Christians must either select alternative means for educating their children, or they will indoctrinate them with anti-Christian Humanist values in public schools.

The public schools have been a major force in the creation of a secularized society, because they have instilled in generations of students the impression that religion is a purely private matter which as no place in public life.[1]

---

1 James Hitchcock, Carl Horn, Ed., *Disentangling the Secular Humanism Debate, Whose Values? The Battle for Morality in Pluralistic America* (Ann Arbor: Servant Books, 1985), 28.

CHRISTIANITY OR HUMANISM

PLAYING WITH FIRE

Mrs. Aimes enthusiastically addressed her seventh graders: "This month we are exploring chapters 3 and 4 in our social studies textbook, *Across the Centuries*. We will discuss the following lessons:

Desert Bloom—Caravan Cities	Muhammad and Islam
Early Islam	A Century of Expansion
The Golden Age	Islamic Spain

We will review key teachings and beliefs of Islam. We will learn about how these beliefs affect the everyday life of Muslims like our new friend Antar. He will come now and demonstrate some of the basic worship forms of his religion."

Julie was fascinated by Antar, and he was to be Mrs. Aimes' assistant for the next few weeks. Julie couldn't wait to get home.

"Mom, Antar gave the most awesome demonstration and report today in social studies!"

"What was it about?"

"His religion. It's so romantic, so spiritual, so awesome!"

"When the fall quarter began last month, you thought Antar was awesome and handsome," observed Mom. "Are you confusing your emotions for him with his religion?"

Julie retorted, "All I know is that Antar visited Christian worship and thought it was boring. I can see why. Today he used his gym mat and showed us how to pray. He taught us to say, 'Allah Akbar' which means 'God is good.' It was awesome!"

"What else did you learn?" asked Mom.

"*Jihad*. It means 'a struggle for spiritual discipline.' It's awesome!"

"Julie, I'm going to make an exception to house rules. You may use the Internet now instead of waiting until your daddy comes home. Google *Jihad* and let's talk when you finish."

After a brief 20 minutes, Julie turned from the computer. "Mom, I don't know what to say. The Twin Towers? That's jihad?"

"Yes, Julie. Jihad is a holy war waged against infidels as a religious duty. And according to their religion, you are an infidel. In

EDUCATION

their view, your faith in Jesus as the Son of God makes you unworthy to live."

"Incidentally," Mom continued, "Google a dictionary and work on building your vocabulary. You've about worn out *awesome* this afternoon."

Why is instruction about Islam permitted in our public classrooms but instruction about Christianity forbidden?

Review Questions

1. How do Christians and Humanists differ in their understandings about philosophical foundations for education?

2. How do Christians and Humanists differ in their objectives for education?

3. How do Christians and Humanists differ in their desired curriculum content of education?

4. How do Christians and Humanists differ in their understandings of authority and responsibility for education?

5. How do Christians and Humanists differ in their understanding of educational administration and instructional methods?

6. What is the significance of religion in Christian education?

7. How do Christians and Humanists differ in understandings of the significance of religion?

8. How do Christians and Humanists differ in their desired results of education?

9. How may Christian education be claimed to be superior to Humanist education?

10. What would our society be like if all our children had a Christian education rather than a Humanist education?

11. What do you think you can do to promote a national system of education based upon Christian ideals?

Suggested Reading in Education

Adams, Blair and Joel Stein. *Who Owns the Children? Compulsory Education and the Dilemma of Ultimate Authority*, Grand Junction, CO: Truth Forum, 1983.

Blumenfeld, Samuel L. *Is Public Education Necessary?* Boise, ID: The Paradigm Co. 1985.

Blumenfeld, Samuel L. *N. E. A.: Trojan Horse In American Education*. Boise, ID: The Paradigm Co. 1984.

Eakman, B. K. *Educating for the New World Order*, Portland: OR: Halcyon House, 1991.

Noebel, David A., J. F. Baldwin and Kevin Bywater. *Clergy in the Classroom: The Religion of Secular Humanism*, Manitou Springs, CO: Summit Press, 1995.

Vitz, Paul C. *Censorship: Evidence of Bias in Our Children's Textbooks*, Ann Arbor, MI: Servant Books, 1986.

CHAPTER 13

CULTURE

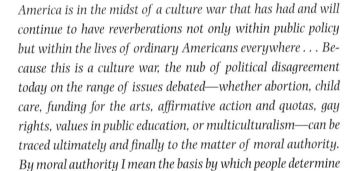

America is in the midst of a culture war that has had and will continue to have reverberations not only within public policy but within the lives of ordinary Americans everywhere... Because this is a culture war, the nub of political disagreement today on the range of issues debated—whether abortion, child care, funding for the arts, affirmative action and quotas, gay rights, values in public education, or multiculturalism—can be traced ultimately and finally to the matter of moral authority. By moral authority I mean the basis by which people determine whether something is good or bad, right or wrong, acceptable or unacceptable, and so on.[1]

The word *culture* is here used to describe the totality of beliefs, actions, and patterns characteristic of a society as a whole or of its various parts, for example, a particular region, social, ethnic, age, or religious group. A Christian culture is one with Christian ideals and behaviors; a Humanist culture is one with Humanist ideals and behaviors. Since all humans are innately religious, then all human cultures have religious foundations and values. Inherent within all cultures are conflicting values. In reality, a completely Christian culture has never existed, nor has a completely

---

1 James Davison Hunter, *Culture Wars: The Struggle to Define* America (New York: Basic Books, 1991), 34, 42.

CHRISTIANITY OR HUMANISM

Humanist culture ever existed. Even so, cultural differences may be broadly contrasted by their ideologies. Arguments may also be given to show that an ideal Christian culture is superior to an ideal Humanist culture.

Contrasting Cultural Worldviews

Christian and Humanist cultures differ in their foundations. A Christian culture generally acquires its ideas from the Bible, specifically from the teachings of Jesus and his apostles. A Humanist culture generally acquires its ideas from Graeco-Roman literature and from Renaissance and Enlightenment thought. Christian culture is theistic and transcendental; Humanist culture is atheistic and altogether human. Christian culture is oriented toward human nature as being both physical and spiritual; Humanist culture is oriented only toward the physical nature of humanity. Christian culture considers reality to encompass both time and eternity; Humanist culture considers reality to be only in time. Humanists think eternity is unreal.

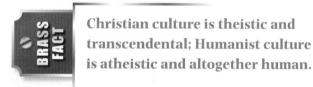

BRASS FACT: Christian culture is theistic and transcendental; Humanist culture is atheistic and altogether human.

Cultural Ideologies

A Christian culture recognizes the sovereignty, superiority, and excellence of God; a Humanist culture believes in the sovereignty and superiority of humanity. A Christian culture grants individuals freedom to pursue social and economic interests; a Humanist culture looks to centralized social and economic control of individuals. A Christian culture requires freedom in context of Christian ethics; a Humanist culture requires freedom from divine revelation. A Christian society is morally stable; a Humanist society fluctuates morally. A Christian culture cultivates personal righteousness; a Humanist culture cultivates the sensual. A Christian society walks in the old paths of the tried and true; a Humanist society seeks the new and the untried. A Christian culture denies religious neutrality while promoting Christian perspectives in all cultural contexts; a Humanist culture affirms secularism and religious neutrality, yet generally acts with anti-Christian bias in all cultural contexts. A Christian culture tends toward economic and political freedom; a Humanist culture tends toward economic and political control.

Cultural Values

Christians respect the elderly, honor marriage, and hate divorce; Humanists extol youth, dishonor marriage, and sanction divorce. Christians exalt parental authority; Humanists exalt civil authority. Christians tend to judge others in relation to their standing with God, family, community, and personal service; Humanists tend to judge others in relation to their wealth, power, position, fame, and personal achievements. Christianity calls for self-denial and esteem of others better than self; Humanism produces selfishness—the valuing self above all else. Because Christianity teaches self-denial, Christians are generally generous toward the needy. Because Humanists value self above all else, many are less inclined to be personally generous toward the needy. Christianity produces a society that emphasizes service to God and fellow human beings; Humanism produces a society that emphasizes personal affluence and personal peace.[1]

Cultural Desires

Christians ideally strive for excellence; Humanists are content with allowing mediocrity. Christians, through religion, push a salvation agenda as a means of community improvement; Humanists seek community improvement through politics and social agen-

---

1 A good statement about these impoverished values in our society is given by Francis Schaeffer, *How Should We Then Live?: The Rise and Decline of Western Culture* (Old Tappan, NJ: Fleming H. Revell Company, 1976), 205.

das. Christians seek God's glory through service; Humanists seek personal glory through wealth, pleasure, fame, and power.

In a Christian culture, an artist's talent is assumed to come from God's endowment; in a Humanist culture, an artist's talent is assumed to come from the naturally endowed genius of the artist.

The Spread of Culture

Media promote culture by art: paintings, sculpture, and architecture. What is the origin of an artist's talent? Is it from God or nature? In a Christian culture, art is often used as a means of glorifying God, and the artist seeks to honor God through excellence in craftsmanship; in a Humanist culture, art is often used as a means of rebellion against God, and the artist seeks self-glorification. In a Christian culture, art is valued primarily for its function and beauty; in a Humanist culture, art is valued primarily for its creativity and independent spirit. In a Christian culture, artists generally identify with their own countries; in a Humanist culture, artists generally feel alienated from their own countries.

Consider the influence of culture by literature: books, journals, and newspapers. In a Christian culture, literature is written with an assumption that absolutes exist, and optimism is based on faith and reason that produce a firm foundation for objectivity. In a Humanist culture, literature is written with the assumption that all things are relative. In Humanist journalism, optimism often comes from non-reason that blurs distinctions between objectivity and subjectivity.

In a Humanist culture, themes for audio visual presentations often ignore, distort, and blaspheme Christianity.

What about audio-visual technology—radio, recordings, drama, movies, and television? In a Christian culture, themes considered for audio-visual presentations generally honor Christian values. They are generally optimistic, showing hope, and displaying both good and evil in the human spirit. In a Humanist culture, themes considered for audio-visual presentations often ignore, distort, and blaspheme Christianity. They are often nihilistic and pessimistic. Horror is often used to prey on the human spirit.

Does the musical media spread cultural values? Absolutely. In a Christian culture, music presents a diverse, yet harmonious, sense of reality that leads to resolution. Music in a Christian culture appeals to humanity's righteous and spiritual nature. In a Humanist culture, music presents a fragmented sense of reality that originated by chance and leads to absurdity.

CULTURE	Biblical Christianity	or	Secular Humanism
Foundation	Teachings of Jesus; theistic and transcendental	or	Teachings from Renaissance thought; humanistic and atheistic
Ideologies	Recognizes sovereignty, superiority, and excellence of God; cultivates righteousness	or	Believes in sovereignty and superiority of mankind; cultivates the sensual
Values	Respects the elderly, honors marriage, hates divorce; exalts parental authority; judges success by spirituality	or	Extols youth, dishonors marriage, sanctions divorce; exalts civil authority; judges success by materialism
Goals	Strives for excellence; seeks community improvements through evangelism; wants God's glory through service	or	Allows mediocrity; seek community improvement through politics; wants personal worldly glory
Media Influence	Talent attributed to God and used for His glory; portrays life as created with order; results in cultural excellence.	or	Talent attributed to nature and used for personal glory; portrays life as evolved from chaos; results in cultural degradation.
SUMMARY	God	or	Man

Why Christian Culture Is Superior

Better Foundations

Is a culture not better when people believe they are spiritual as well as physical, they will have an eternal existence after passing through this lifetime, and they will be held accountable by God for their behavior in this life? Will not these beliefs serve to check improper behavior and make for a society that is more amiable?

Better Ideologies

Is a culture not better when people believe in the sovereignty of God, when they are individually free to pursue their own dreams, when they live in communities that are morally stable, and when everyone strives for personal righteousness? Is it not better to live in such a society than in one where people have freedoms restricted, that is constantly changing its moral standards, and where the idea of living better is not generally considered?

Better Values

Is a culture not better when the elderly are honored, when marriage commitments endure, where divorce is considered disgraceful, where children are loved, where people are esteemed for their righteous standing with God, and where people are voluntarily generous toward the needy? These values that promote peace, honor, and kindness are surely better than discordant values of disrespect, disharmony, and unconcern toward others that characterize non-Christian societies.

Better Motivations

Is a culture not better when its people strive for excellence in their work, when people are concerned for the eternal soul salvation of their friends and neighbors, and when service toward others is considered a high calling? Are not the motivations of love better than not caring about the physical and spiritual well-being of others?

Better Understandings of God, Man, and Nature

Is a culture not better when it recognizes the existence of God and acts like it is accountable to God, when it portrays nature as having come from God, when it looks upon art as a means of glorifying God, and when it is valued for its realism and beauty? Is a culture not better when its media portray life as having been created with order rather than chaos? Is a culture not better when its media assume the existence of absolute values? Is a culture not better when it seeks to portray reality with hope and optimism, although it may see both good and bad in human realities? Is a culture not better when its music is uplifting rather than degrading, and when it promotes righteous rather than debasing behavior?

Conclusion

Since a Christian culture is superior to a Humanist culture, then Christians should be actively engaged in promoting stronger Christian values within their cultures. Surely this is what Jesus meant when He declared that Christians are the salt of the earth, the light of the world, a city set on a hill (Matthew 5:13–16), and a leavening influence (Matthew 13:33; Luke 13:21; 1 Corinthians 5:7–8; Galatians 5:9). Christians must be active, leading whenever possible, not only in the work of the church through evangelism, edification, and benevolence, but also in every other sphere of their cultures. This includes every place where Christian ideals and behaviors occur within a culture—whether in a culture's institutions such as the home, civil government, church, workplace, volunteer organizations, or in personal leisure time activities such as hobbies, recreational activities, and social or political interactions.

Since some people do not favor Christian values, then Christians may expect opposition to their efforts to build a Christian culture. "All who desire to live godly in Christ Jesus will suffer persecution" (2 Timothy 3:12). Christians, however, are not afraid. "For God has not given us a spirit of fear, but of power and of love and of a sound mind" (2 Timothy 1:7). Christians should seek a godly environment in which to live now, and an eternal home when this life is over. To achieve these values, Christians should be ready, at least ideally, to sacrifice their wealth, time, energy, and even their very lives because heavenly values are realized to be superior to earthly values.

In sociology, the blending into culture is called the "socialization process." That process is the means by which one becomes a functioning member of society, reflecting the values and behavior of the culture. The only way to avoid that process is with a strong confrontation. God has not called us to the status quo, to personal peace and affluence, but to conflict and confrontation with society . . . The Christian who confronts his culture becomes a marginal person of that culture, a person on the rim, who in many ways no longer fits, especially in a culture that has reverted to pagan thought. And yet, in Scripture this is the position to which God has called us: "If the world hate you, you know that it hated me before it hated you. If you were of the world, the world would love its own; but because you are not of the world, but I have chosen you out of the world, therefore the world hates you" (John 15:18–19 NASB).[1]

PLAYING WITH FIRE

Mrs. Noles didn't know why Dr. Jan Whitecut was fidgety. The visit was routine. But then the doctor painted a clear picture with a single question: "Whitney, I need you to lie down on this table. Shall I ask Mrs. Noles to leave?"

Fifteen-year-old Whitney looked wide-eyed at Dr. Jan Whitecut and asked spunkily: "Why would I want her to leave? She's my mother!"

A sheepish look enveloped the gynecologist's face, but she recovered immediately and responded curtly: "I always ask a parent

---

1 Richard A. Fowler and H. Wayne House, *The Christian Confronts His Culture: Right to Life, Feminism, Homosexuality* (Chicago: Moody Press, 1983), xi–xii.

CULTURE

or guardian to remain in the waiting room. My conversation with you, by law, is confidential."

"I need my mother's support and guidance, Dr. Whitecut. "I don't see a problem with her being in here."

"As you wish," the doctor conceded. Then she began her questions. "Are you sexually active? Do you plan to be? Are you taking contraceptives?"

The doctor then proceeded to explain about the sexually transmitted disease, human papillomavirus (HPV), and the vaccine GARDASIL that was on the market. "HPV causes genital warts that often lead to cervical cancer in young women," she explained.

"What causes HPV?" Whitney asked. The question brought a smile to Mrs. Noles' face.

"Sexual contact with an infected person," answered Dr. Whitecut.

"So if I don't have sex until I marry, I won't need the vaccine? Right?" queried Whitney.

"Right," answered the doctor.

"Well, then, I don't need it." Whitney hesitated, then continued. "And I want my mom to be able to give her input any time she chooses!"

Who is more qualified for this type of decision making—parents or children? Contrast Humanistic and Christian morality: vaccine control vs. God control.

Review Questions

1. How do philosophical foundations of a Christian culture differ from philosophical foundations of a Humanist culture?

2. How do Christian cultural ideologies differ from Humanist cultural ideologies?

3. How do Christian cultural values differ from Humanist cultural values?

4. How do Christian cultural desires differ from Humanist cultural desires?

5. How do media in art, literature, theater, and music in a Christian culture differ from the same media in a Humanist culture?

6. How may Christian culture be said to be superior to a Humanist culture?

7. What do you think you can best do to promote a thoroughly Christian culture?

Suggested Readings in Culture

Bennett, William J. *The Index of Leading Cultural Indicators: Facts and Figures on the State of American Society*, New York: Simon and Schuster, 1994.

Dobson, James and Gary L. Bauer. *Children at Risk*, Dallas: Word Publishing, 1990

Senior, John. *The Death of Christian Culture*, Harrison, NY: RC Books, 1978.

SUMMARY

Christian religion is superior because . . .

- Christian religion is consistent with Christian beliefs; Humanist religion is not consistent with Humanist beliefs.
- Christian religion has better answers to questions of identity than does Humanist religion.

Christian philosophy is superior because . . .

- Christian philosophy is consistent with its perception of how things can be known; Humanist philosophy is inconsistent with its rules for acquiring knowledge.
- Christian philosophy is more reasonable than Humanist philosophy.
- Christian philosophy is more consistent with natural sciences than is Humanist philosophy.

Christian history is superior because . . .

- Christian history, unlike Humanist history, is consistent with its ideology.
- Christian history fits the actual historical and scientific facts; the theory of evolution, the basis of Humanist history, does not.
- Christian history gives a solid basis for assessment of the future; Humanist history does not.

Christian ethics is superior because . . .

- Christian ethics is inherently harmonious; Humanist ethics produces tensions.
- Christian ethics succeeds as a foundation for building an abiding society; Humanist ethics does not.
- Christian ethics requires personal responsibility toward others; Humanist ethics does not.
- Christian ethics has grounds for establishing truth and goodness; Humanist ethics has no authoritative foundation for establishing truth or goodness.

Christian biology is superior because . . .

- Christian biology gives a better explanation for reproduction of life than does Humanist biology.
- Christian biology is more supportable by the known facts of science than is Humanist biology.
- Christian biology gives a better explanation of nature than does Humanist biology.
- Christian biology provides a better foundation for living than does Humanist biology.

Christian medicine is superior because . . .

- Christian medicine has greater respect for human life than does Humanist medicine.
- Christian medicine has absolute moral standards that produce better societies; Humanist medicine does not.

Christian psychology is superior because . . .

- Christian psychology is consistent with its philosophical foundations; Humanist psychology is not.
- Christian psychology gives better explanations of human nature and behavior than does Humanist psychology.

Christian sociology is superior because. . .

- Christian sociology produces a stable society; Humanist sociology does not.
- Christian sociology operates on fixed standards; Humanist sociology does not.
- Christian sociology emphasizes individual social responsibilities; Humanist sociology does not.

Christian law is superior because . . .

- Christian law, being absolute, produces order; Humanist law, being relative, tends to produce social disorder and immorality.
- Christian law alone provides a universal standard for ascertaining justice.

SUMMARY

- Christian law provides better human rights and demands greater responsibilities than does Humanist law.

Christian politics is superior because . . .

- Christian politics is more consistent with natural social and economic realities than is Humanist law.
- Christian politics grants more individual and religious freedoms than does Humanist politics.
- Christian politics is based on absolute precepts given by God in Scripture; Humanist politics is based on relative human ideas.
- Christian politics, unlike Humanist politics, produces societies wherein there is less crime.

Christian economics is superior because . . .

- Christian economics creates greater wealth and prosperity than does Humanist economics.
- Christian economics grants greater personal and economic freedoms than does Humanist economics.

Christian education is superior because . . .

- Christian education produces greater moral results than does Humanist education.
- Christian education produces greater intellectual results than does Humanist education.
- Christian education is consistent with the system of free enterprise; Humanist education is not.
- Christian education requires that the Christian religion be the foundation upon which all of life is based.
- Christian education produces an awareness of eternity.

Christian culture is superior because . . .

- Christian culture has a better foundation.
- Christian culture has better ideologies.
- Christian culture has better values.
- Christian culture has better motivations.
- Christian culture better portrays God, man, and nature.

WHAT CHRISTIANS CAN DO

Inform Yourself and Others

- Collect names, addresses, phone numbers, and other pertinent information of public officials and other contact persons to whom you may write.
- Learn all you can about moral, political, social, cultural, and other issues confronting Christians. Read journals, books, and other related material in order to learn the facts. Be willing to spend time and money to learn.
- Listen to special radio talk shows. Watch pertinent television programs which deal with issues.
- Join educational and activist organizations whose purposes are both to inform and to participate in the political process, but join those which share your values. You can learn pertinent information on timely issues from groups like Christian Coalition and Eagle Forum.
- Share what you learn, especially your journals, books, videos and other materials with friends, neighbors and/or church groups.

Mold Public Opinion

- Write letters and telegrams, make phone calls and send faxes to public officials, businesses, editors, and other influential people. Be sure you know what you are talking about. Give good arguments, and back them up with evidence. Address only one issue per letter or call. Make your point short and quick.
- Make speeches in appropriate public forums. Call radio talk shows to express the Christian perspective and to show how it is superior to all others. Write articles for publications.
- Learn how to be persuasive in both speaking and writing.

Shape Public Policy

- Vote in every public election, whether local, statewide, or national.
- Become a leader in some influential sphere. Get into a position to help shape public policy where it counts. Use your influence to affect changes in policy-making boards and positions of all types: city councils, county commissioners, state and national legislators, legal and judicial positions, gubernatorial and presidential positions, etc. Become a leader in journalism, medicine, or some other profession.
- Develop and/or participate in a communication system to inform others and activate contacts when special issues arise and need immediate attention.
- Organize and/or join organizations already formed whose values you share. Larger organizations and networks of organizations have greater political clout.

Demonstrate Christian Values

- Demonstrate godly manners, morals, and values in both speech and behavior on all occasions with all persons.
- Be compassionate, individually and collectively, especially toward the poor and the oppressed. The grace of God must flow through Christians to voluntarily assist the needy, both physically and spiritually.
- Always operate within the law, unless it conflicts with the word of God.

SUGGESTED READINGS

Basic Documents of Humanism By Humanists

(You can probably find these on the Internet)

Humanist Manifesto I, drafted by Roy Wood Sellers, first published in *The New Humanist*, May/June, 1993 (Vol. VI, No. 3), co-signed by 34 persons, of which the first and most prominent was John Dewey.

Humanist Manifesto II, drafted by Paul Kurtz and Edwin H. Wilson, first published in *The Humanist*, Sept/Oct, 1973 (Vol. XXXIII, No. 5), co-signed by 114 prominent persons, including Isaac Asimov, Edd Doerr, Antony Flew, Sidney Hook, Corliss Lamont, Lester Kirkendall, and B. F. Skinner.

Humanism and Its Aspirations, subtitled as *Manifesto III*, a successor to the *Humanist Manifesto* of 1933, apparently written by committees of the American Humanist Association, first published in *The Humanist*, May/June, 2003, signed by over 90 prominent persons, including 21 Nobel Laureats.

A Secular Humanist Declaration, drafted by Paul Kurtz, first published in *Free Inquiry*, Winter, 1980/1981, (Vol. 1, No. 1), co-signed by 81 persons from eight countries.

A Declaration of Interdependence: A New Global Ethics, drafted by Paul Kurtz, first published in *Free Inquiry*, Fall, 1988 (Vol. 8, No. 4), endorsed by 14 Humanist Laureates of the Academy of Humanism, the Board of Directors of the International Humanists and Ethical Union, and the International Humanists and Ethical Union.

Books By Non-Humanists

(You can probably acquire these books through inner-library loans from your local public library.)

Chambers, Claire. *The SIECUS CIRCLE: A Humanist Revolution*, Belmont, MASS: Western Islands. 1977.

Colson, Charles and Nancy Pearcy. *How Now Shall We Live?* Wheaton, IL: Tyndale House Publishers, Inc. 1999.

Geisler, Norman L. *Is Man The Measure? An Evaluation of Contemporary Humanism,* Grand Rapids, MI: Baker Book House, 1983.

Hightower, Terry M. *Embattled Christianity: A Call To Alarm The Church To Humanism,* The Third Annual Shenandoah Lectures, Shenandoah Church of Christ, 11026 Wurzbach Rd., Austin, TX 78230, 1989.

Hitchcock, James. *What Is Secular Humanism? Why Humanism Became Secular and How It Is Changing Our World,* Ann Arbor, MI: Servant Books, 1982.

Hunter, James Davison, *Culture Wars: The Struggle to Define America,* New York: HarperCollins, 1991.

Noebel, David A. *Understanding the Times: The Story of the Biblical Christian, Marxist/Leninist and Secular Humanist Worldviews,* Manitou Springs, CO: Summit Press, 1991.

Schaeffer, Francis A. *How Should We Then Live? The Rise and Decline of Western Thought and Culture,* Old Tappan, NJ: Fleming H. Revell Company, 1976.

Schlossberg, Herbert. *Idols for Destruction: Christian Faith and Its Confrontation with American Society,* Nashville: Thomas Nelson Publishers, 1983.

Name Index

An Inquiry into the Nature and Causes of the Wealth of Nations 129
Anselm 38
Blackstone, William 114
Blamires, Harry 10
Bylaws of the American Humanist Association 19, 21
Comte, August 23
Darwin, Charles 68, 87
Das Kapital 129
Dewey, John 139, 147, 166
Freud, Sigmund 87
Hardeman, Dr. Pat 8
Hobbs, Lottie Beth 7, 21
Humanist Manifesto I 11, 18, 24, 25, 28, 29, 30, 68, 166
Humanist Manifesto II 19, 26, 27, 29, 30, 60, 68, 102, 166
Mann, Horace 139, 147
Marx, Karl 129
Noebel, David A. 7, 8, 39, 50, 54, 140, 150, 167
Pro-Family Forum 7, 21
Skinner, B. F. 88, 166
Slate, Dr. Phillip 8
Smith, Adam 129
The Christian Mind: How Should a Christian Think? 10
The Release of the Destruction of Life Devoid of Value 81
Thompson, Dr. Bert 8
Torcaso v. Watkins 20
Understanding the Times: The Story of the Biblical Christian, Marxist / Leninist, and Secular Humanist Worldviews 7, 39, 50, 54, 167
Watson, John B. 88
Wundt, Wilhelm 87

Scripture Index

Genesis 1:1 68, 141
Genesis 1:24-31 68
Genesis 1:26-27 29
Genesis 2:7 29
Genesis 3:5-6 22
Genesis 3:19 29
Genesis 3:20 29
Genesis 9:2-3, 6 29
Genesis 9:6 29
Genesis 11:4-7 22

Exodus 20 63
Exodus 20:15 133
Exodus 22:1, 4 111

Deuteronomy 5 63
Deuteronomy 7:12-15 134
Deuteronomy 28 52
Deuteronomy 28:1-8 134

1 Kings 21:1-14 133

Psalm 8:3-4 68
Psalm 8:5 29
Psalm 14:1 25
Psalm 24:1 132
Psalm 53:1 25

Proverbs 1:7 141
Proverbs 2:6 141

Ecclesiastes 11:9 30
Ecclesiastes 12:14 30

Ezekiel 28:2 22

Matthew 5-7 63
Matthew 5:13-16 157
Matthew 13:33 157
Matthew 20:26-28 91
Matthew 25:21, 23 30
Matthew 25:31-46 30

Luke 13:21 157

John 1:1-4 39
John 1:3 68

John 1:12-13 29
John 1:14 35
John 3:6 91
John 5:28-29 30
John 13:14-15 91
John 15:18-19 158

Acts 17:26 29
Acts 17:30-31 30
Acts 20:35 135

Romans 1:21-32 91
Romans 3:10, 23 100
Romans 6:21 91
Romans 6:23 30
Romans 7:6 92
Romans 8:5-8 91
Romans 8:6 91
Romans 8:9-14 91
Romans 8:37 91
Romans 12:1, 8 91
Romans 12:8 135
Romans 12:11 92
Romans 13:4 110, 123
Romans 14:18 92

1 Corinthians 3:3 91
1 Corinthians 3:16 91
1 Corinthians 5:7-8 157
1 Corinthians 6:9-10 91
1 Corinthians 6:19 91
1 Corinthians 9:19 30
1 Corinthians 15:48 91
1 Corinthians 15:57 91

2 Corinthians 2:14 91

Galatians 3:26 29
Galatians 4:6 91
Galatians 5:9 157
Galatians 5:13 30, 92
Galatians 6:10 135

Ephesians 2:3, 5 91
Ephesians 2:12 91
Ephesians 3:9 68
Ephesians 3:16 91
Ephesians 4:22 91
Ephesians 4:28 135

Ephesians 6:1-4 144
Ephesians 6:5-8 92

Philippians 2:17 92

Colossians 1:11 91
Colossians 1:16 68
Colossians 2:6-10 44
Colossians 2:18 91
Colossians 3:5 91
Colossians 3:17 118

1 Thessalonians 1:7-9 30
1 Thessalonians 1:9 30

2 Thessalonians 1:7-9 30
2 Thessalonians 3:10 133

1 Timothy 5:8 122

2 Timothy 1:7 91, 157
2 Timothy 3:12 157

Titus 3:3 91

Hebrews 1:2 68
Hebrews 2:7, 9 29
Hebrews 9:14 92
Hebrews 9:27 30
Hebrews 11:28 30
Hebrews 12:28 92

James 1:5 141
James 2:13-16 100
James 4:4 91

1 Peter 2:14 110, 123
1 Peter 4:3 91

2 Peter 2:10 91

1 John 4:4 91
1 John 5:4 91
1 John 5:19 91

Revelation 12:11 91

Subject Index

A

abortion 23, 79, 81, 82, 102, 108, 151
absolute standards 103, 124
age of enlightenment 14
American Humanist Association 19, 21, 166
anthropic principle 38, 39, 44
art 154, 157, 160
atheism 19
audio-visual technology 155
autonomy 26, 97, 102, 142

B

basic unit of society 122
Bible 14, 24, 36, 37, 39, 44, 50, 51, 52, 57, 93, 97, 108, 110, 130, 152
    accuracy 39, 50, 52
    archeology 52
    authority 25, 59, 60, 61, 63, 73, 83, 84, 98, 99, 100, 107, 122, 124, 133, 135, 137, 140, 142, 144, 145, 149, 151, 153
    Christianity 7, 8, 9, 10, 11, 13, 14, 15, 16, 17, 20, 24, 26, 27, 28, 33, 44, 62, 77, 82, 87, 94, 102, 114, 116, 137, 139, 149, 153, 154, 155, 167
    history 9, 10, 14, 15, 22, 35, 36, 40, 41, 47, 48, 49, 50, 51, 52, 53, 54, 55, 56, 73, 97, 115, 129, 137, 161
biogenesis 72
birth control 102

C

capitalism 15, 99, 129, 130, 131, 132, 133, 135, 136, 137
centralized control 132
chance 25, 30, 42, 50, 51, 53, 61, 68, 69, 72, 89, 92, 155
Christian 7, 9, 10, 11, 13, 14, 15, 16, 17, 19, 20, 22, 23, 26, 28, 31, 33, 35, 36, 39, 41, 42, 43, 44, 45, 47, 48, 49, 50, 51, 53, 54, 55, 56, 57, 58, 59, 60, 61, 62, 63, 64, 65, 66, 67, 68, 71, 72, 73, 75, 78, 79, 80, 81, 82, 83, 85, 87, 88, 89, 92, 94, 95, 96, 97, 98, 99, 100, 101, 102, 103, 104, 105, 106, 107, 108, 109, 110, 111, 112, 113, 114, 115, 116, 117, 118, 119, 120, 122, 123, 124, 125, 127, 128, 130, 133, 134, 135, 137, 138, 140, 141, 142, 143, 144, 145, 146, 147, 148, 149, 150, 151, 152, 153, 154, 155, 156, 157, 158, 159, 160, 161, 162, 163, 164, 165, 167
church 7, 8, 10, 29, 41, 66, 97, 98, 99, 100, 105, 110, 119, 120, 127, 131, 139, 147, 157, 164, 167
civil governments 99, 118, 119, 121, 122, 127, 131, 132, 133, 135, 139, 140, 144
civil liberties 102, 103
communism 130, 136
consciousness 89
contingent beings 38, 40
cosmology 36, 40, 44, 45
creation 15, 16, 25, 29, 39, 40, 47, 48, 51, 52, 53, 54, 67, 68, 71, 72, 73, 74, 75, 107, 108, 109, 114, 141, 147
    doctrine of 67, 70, 141

crime 110, 111, 112, 115, 124, 163
criminal rights 111
crusades 82
cryonics 83
culture 8, 9, 10, 14, 15, 84, 103, 114, 151, 152, 153, 154, 155, 156, 157, 158, 159, 160, 163
    cultural desires 153, 160
    cultural foundations 140
    cultural ideologies 152
    cultural values 155, 159

D

democratic socialism 130
divorce 23, 102, 103, 153, 155, 156
DNA genetic information 38
dualism 16, 95

E

economics 5, 16, 99, 101, 111, 116, 128, 129, 134, 138
    economic planning 131, 132
    economic systems 129, 137
    economic welfare 132, 133, 135
    global economy 132
    poverty 97, 106, 131, 135
    private ownership 121, 130
    prosperity 17, 131, 132, 134, 146, 163
education 9, 14, 20, 62, 73, 93, 99, 129, 133, 134, 137, 139, 140, 141, 142, 143, 144, 145, 146, 147, 149, 150, 151, 163
    curriculum content 141
    educational aims 140
    educational methodology 142
    educational results 143
    government schools 99, 100, 143
    moral education 62
    public education 20, 129, 139, 140, 142, 151
egalitarianism 14, 133
entitlements 135
environmental adaptations 71
epistemology 36, 40, 41, 42, 43, 44, 45
equality 82, 102, 131, 134, 141
eschatology 53
eternal destiny 14, 25, 26, 30, 41, 48, 146
eternity 29, 89, 146, 152, 163
ethics 5, 16, 57, 60, 62, 63, 66, 83, 166
    ethical foundations 57, 63
euthanasia 77, 79, 81, 82, 84, 85, 102
evolution 14, 15, 28, 40, 42, 51, 52, 53, 61, 67, 68, 69, 70, 71, 72, 73, 75, 87, 92, 109, 114, 137, 141, 142, 145, 161
    evolutionary presuppositions 124
    macro-evolution 72
    theistic evolution 68, 69

F

family 80, 82, 83, 84, 97, 98, 99, 100, 101, 102, 103, 105, 110, 111, 113, 115, 119, 121, 122, 124, 126, 134, 145, 153
fascism 130
feminism 14, 141, 145, 158
first amendment 20, 32
first cause 24
forgiveness 60, 63, 90
fossil record 70, 75
Foundations of Society 98
freedom 17, 43, 49, 60, 61, 88, 90, 92, 98, 99, 102, 123, 132, 134, 152, 153
free enterprise 80, 82, 83, 129, 163
free will 49, 50, 88, 89, 98, 99

G

globalism 14, 15, 16, 133
guaranteed minimum annual wage 99
guilt 58, 90, 92, 93, 96

H

hedonism 14, 141, 145
history 5, 9, 10, 13, 14, 15, 16, 22, 35, 36, 40, 41, 47, 48, 49, 50, 51, 52, 53, 54, 55, 56, 73, 81, 97, 115, 129, 143, 161
   origin of history 48
   progression of history 48
human 10, 11, 13, 14, 15, 18, 24, 25, 26, 27, 29, 30, 36, 37, 40, 48, 49, 50, 51, 52, 53, 57, 58, 59, 60, 61, 63, 64, 67, 68, 69, 72, 77, 78, 79, 81, 82, 83, 84, 85, 87, 88, 89, 90, 92, 93, 95, 98, 102, 104, 107, 108, 109, 112, 113, 114, 117, 119, 121, 123, 125, 131, 132, 134, 140, 141, 145, 146, 151, 152, 153, 155, 157, 159, 162, 163
   human environment 50
   human life 11, 15, 60, 61, 77, 79, 81, 82, 83, 84, 98, 102, 162
   human potential 90
   human progress 50, 51
   Human reason 112
Humanism 2, 7, 8, 9, 11, 13, 14, 15, 16, 17, 18, 19, 20, 21, 22, 23, 24, 25, 26, 27, 28, 29, 30, 31, 32, 33, 36, 38, 42, 45, 51, 57, 58, 61, 62, 67, 71, 72, 78, 82, 88, 93, 95, 100, 101, 102, 103, 104, 109, 110, 111, 112, 113, 116, 120, 121, 123, 125, 126, 127, 131, 133, 134, 137, 139, 140, 141, 145, 147, 150, 153, 155, 166, 167
humanism 2
humanists 9, 10, 11, 13, 14, 15, 16, 17, 18, 19, 20, 21, 24, 25, 26, 27, 28, 29, 30, 31, 33, 36, 37, 40, 41, 42, 45, 47, 48, 49, 50, 51, 52, 53, 55, 61, 62, 63, 67, 68, 69, 72, 75, 77, 78, 79, 80, 83, 88, 89, 90, 91, 92, 93, 95, 96, 98, 99, 100, 101, 102, 103, 104, 105, 107, 108, 109, 110, 111, 112, 113, 115, 119, 120, 121, 123, 124, 127, 130, 131, 132, 133, 140, 141, 142, 149, 152, 153, 154, 166

I

ideologies 47, 50, 55, 77, 118, 152, 155, 156, 159, 163
illiteracy rate 143

SUBJECT INDEX

image of God 29, 58, 78, 88, 89, 90, 94, 146
Immortality 26, 27
incest 80, 108
infanticide 79, 81, 82

J

Jesus 17, 24, 26, 27, 29, 35, 41, 44, 50, 53, 55, 118, 149, 152, 155, 157
judges 32, 127
justice 10, 16, 59, 60, 62, 63, 99, 109, 111, 113, 114, 116, 118, 119, 120, 122, 123, 125, 132, 162

L

law 5, 9, 14, 16, 24, 38, 44, 58, 59, 61, 72, 73, 84, 93, 97, 98, 104, 107, 108, 109, 110, 111, 112, 113, 114, 115, 116, 118, 119, 120, 123, 124, 159, 162, 163, 165
    legal absolutes 109
    legal foundations 108
    legal functions 108
    legal practitioners 114
    legal purposes 109
    natural law 115
literature 87, 103, 152, 154, 160
love 3, 35, 59, 60, 63, 104, 119, 124, 156, 157, 158

M

marijuana 80
marriage 83, 99, 101, 111, 126, 153, 155, 156
materialism 14, 36, 37, 44, 78, 141, 145, 155
media 73, 87, 126, 154, 155, 157, 160
medicine 5, 14, 16, 73, 77, 78, 79, 80, 81, 82, 83, 85, 93, 162, 165
mental functions 89
mental health 81, 90, 95
mind-altering drugs 80
monism 16, 95
morality 10, 48, 49, 57, 58, 60, 62, 140, 145, 147, 159
    moral character 143
    moral education 62
    moral permissiveness 62
    moral purity 83, 124
    moral standards 52, 83, 156, 162
multiculturalism 14, 133, 141, 145, 151
music 155, 157, 160
mutations 68, 69, 71, 73, 75

N

nation 7, 17, 98, 110, 114, 130, 140
naturalism 14, 16, 24, 27, 36, 37, 43, 44, 73, 78, 92, 145
natural selection 69, 70, 71, 75, 145
nature 23, 24, 25, 26, 27, 28, 29, 31, 33, 35, 36, 37, 38, 40, 41, 42, 47, 48, 51, 55, 58, 61, 62, 70, 72, 73, 78, 82, 83, 88, 89, 90, 91, 92, 93, 105, 110, 124, 125, 127, 129, 131, 134, 141, 144, 145, 146, 152, 154, 155, 157, 162, 163

spiritual nature 24, 36, 47, 82, 88, 89, 91, 124, 141, 146, 155
necessary beings 40

O

ontology 36, 37, 40, 44, 45

P

parental approval 80
philosophy 5, 7, 8, 14, 16, 21, 35, 36, 39, 41, 42, 43, 44, 45, 47, 51, 53, 54, 55, 73, 78, 82, 99, 161
    metaphysical philosophy 35, 36
politics 5, 9, 14, 16, 74, 97, 98, 117, 118, 119, 120, 122, 123, 124, 125, 127, 153, 155, 163
    political goals 121
    political perspectives 117
positive thinking 94
pro-family 80, 82, 97, 126
psychological perspectives 89, 92, 95
psychology 5, 14, 16, 73, 87, 88, 89, 90, 92, 93, 94, 95, 96, 103, 162
public ownership 121, 130
public policies 97, 98, 109, 110, 112
public schools 20, 22, 139, 147
punishment 26, 30, 110, 111, 112, 115, 142

Q

quality of life 78

R

rationalism 14, 24, 27, 36, 37, 43, 44
reason 13, 17, 28, 36, 37, 38, 39, 40, 41, 43, 58, 60, 61, 65, 70, 73, 108, 112, 125, 131, 154
redemption 29, 47, 53, 54, 92, 93
redistribution of wealth 101, 121, 134
rehabilitation 111
relative standards 103
relativism 14, 141
religion 5, 10, 13, 14, 15, 16, 17, 18, 19, 20, 21, 22, 23, 24, 25, 26, 27, 28, 29, 30, 31, 32, 33, 60, 67, 73, 83, 94, 96, 103, 116, 120, 139, 140, 141, 146, 147, 148, 149, 150, 153, 161, 163
    religion of humanity 23
    religious assumptions 21, 31, 146
    religious education 146
    religious foundations 31, 151
    religious humanism 30
renaissance humanism 13, 22
responsibility 8, 27, 61, 63, 83, 100, 101, 102, 103, 117, 118, 132, 135, 142, 149, 161
revelation 9, 10, 24, 26, 28, 36, 37, 38, 40, 41, 43, 45, 68, 69, 70, 88, 92, 108, 140, 146, 152
    general revelation 108
rights 2, 60, 61, 63, 64, 65, 79, 102, 103, 111, 113, 115, 131, 134, 135, 142, 151, 163

SUBJECT INDEX

role of teachers 141
romanticism 14

S

salvation 24, 25, 26, 27, 49, 51, 53, 125, 153, 156
sanctity of life 78, 124
science 26, 27, 28, 37, 38, 39, 42, 43, 69, 73, 75, 77, 80, 98, 162
   scientific issues 85
   scientific method 36, 37, 42, 43
scientism 14, 24, 27, 36, 37, 43, 44, 78
second law of thermodynamics 38, 44, 72
secular education 141, 147
secularism 14, 139, 141, 145, 153
self-actualization 23
self-worship 94, 96, 103
selfishness 23
separation of church and state 100
sexual orientation 80
social 10, 14, 15, 23, 25, 37, 59, 61, 62, 82, 85, 91, 93, 97, 98, 99, 100, 101, 102, 103, 104, 105, 106, 111, 112, 121, 122, 140, 148, 151, 152, 153, 157, 162, 163, 164
   behavior 15, 49, 52, 53, 58, 59, 60, 61, 72, 87, 92, 93, 109, 119, 121, 156, 157, 158, 162, 165
   beliefs 10, 11, 13, 14, 15, 19, 20, 28, 30, 31, 40, 41, 42, 43, 88, 100, 101, 111, 148, 151, 156, 161
   benefits 11, 77, 103, 104
   determinism 43
   issues 66, 78, 79, 80, 83
   responsibilities 60, 63, 98, 100, 102, 103, 113, 119, 162, 163
   social benefits 103
   social issues 80
   social responsibilities 103
   social values 14, 82, 97, 99, 100, 101, 102, 103, 104, 106
socialism 16, 99, 101, 129, 132
sociology 5, 16, 97, 101, 102, 106
   sociological norms 103
spanish inquisition 82
spontaneous generation 38, 44, 68, 69, 70, 71, 75
State 19, 83, 84, 97, 98, 99, 100, 101, 104, 105, 110, 112, 113, 117, 119, 120, 122, 123, 125, 127, 128, 130, 131, 132, 133, 134, 135, 137, 139, 140, 141, 144, 145, 147, 160
statism 14, 139
suffering 90, 93
suicide 79, 82, 102
supernaturalism 16, 70, 71, 78, 141

T

taxation 113, 121, 123, 129, 133, 134
truth 20, 32, 35, 36, 40, 44, 54, 55, 59, 60, 63, 119, 144, 146, 150, 161

U

universal standard 113, 162

V

values
   9, 11, 13, 14, 15, 21, 24, 60, 63, 66, 82, 88, 94, 95, 97, 98, 99, 100, 101, 102, 103, 104, 105, 106, 120, 121, 122, 123, 124, 125, 129, 137, 140, 141, 142, 143, 145, 147, 151, 153, 155, 156, 157, 158, 159, 160, 163, 164, 165

victims' rights 111

W

work ethic 131, 132, 134